Daddy Was a Deacon

Daddy was a Deacon

Connie Moore Hunt

BROADMAN PRESS • Nashville, Tennessee

To
MOTHER,
DAVID,
and
VIRGINIA
who, with me, were Daddy's Oklahoma,
Southern Baptist family

© 1961 • BROADMAN PRESS
Nashville, Tennessee

Second Printing

424-09047

Library of Congress catalog card number: 61-17071
Printed in the United States of America
3.5AL6213

Contents

Prelude

It was hot for May in Fort Worth that afternoon, but there was no escaping the visit to McLean Junior High School. Beth would be enrolled there next year, and this was a special visit for all the sixth-grade children, a sort of preview.

It was most successful. According to Beth, the boys were not "juvenile." They whistled and called you beautiful.

I sighed and reminded myself for the thousandth time that this was a perfectly normal reaction. I really did have a child as tall as I was, and she was very close to teen age. Beth looked quite junior highish in her polished white cotton circle skirt, her red- and white-striped blouse and red cinch belt. I had finished the skirt the night before at some unearthly hour. I was too tired to notice exactly when. But so far so good.

Beth was joyously humming a melody pouring from the car radio, and I began to sing the words to the tune. "Mother!" asked Beth, "Do you know that song? I thought you didn't like that kind of music!"

I laughed. "I did when I was in junior high. That's one of the songs we used to sing. What you're hearing is a new arrangement." The song brought memories. I have special melodies for almost every memory—hymns for Sunday, school songs, chants at football games, and the winsome notes of love. My life has been filled with music and joy, I thought, as I turned the car into the driveway. It was good to have my daughter entering the fulness of just such joy.

We stepped gratefully into the coolness of the house. "Anne," I called, "where are you?" Since first graders got out at two-thirty, Anne should have been home for some time.

From a neighbor's house Anne came running and breathlessly handed me a note. "It's important, Mother," she said. "It's im-*merg*ency. I took this paper over to the neighbor to write down what the lady said on the phone."

The paper had a large number eight scrawled on it in Anne's best first-grade penmanship. In a neighbor's script was "opera-tor" above and "Dallas" below.

I tried to return the call. The long distance operator was kind, but she assured me there was no operator eight in Dallas. They would check with Dallas, however, and let me know.

I hung up wondering at myself for being so anxious. Anne could have been mistaken about an emergency. After all, it is awfully exciting to get a long distance call when you are only six years old and all alone in the house. It was probably a call for Boyd about a weekend preaching appointment. Or some call from Baptist headquarters in Dallas. I would call back and tell the operator to let it go.

When I reached for the phone, it rang. There was no record in Dallas of any call to our number. I thanked her, gave Anne a hug, and said it was good of her to get the message, but it must have been a mix-up somehow.

"Mother," said Anne, "I know it was im-*merg*ency—operator eight, Dallas." I started to have her repeat the polite phrase "Mother, I *think* you are mistaken" when the telephone inter-rupted.

"Mrs. Hunt," said the girl, "this is the switchboard operator at Southwestern Baptist Seminary. I wanted to be sure Dr. Hunt had his emergency call from Altus. He was to call operator eight as soon as possible."

My heart felt as if it needed more room. "Are you sure it was for *Dr.* Hunt?" I asked. She was certain, so I assured her I would see that it was taken care of.

Altus. Of course! Anne often got the two names mixed. I

should have known. The two older children always teased her about confusing "Big D" with the little city in Oklahoma where my parents lived. My mind was racing. And, as usual, I thought of the worst things first. Why would the call go to Boyd? My sister and her husband also lived in Altus, but when they or the folks called, it was to the house, station-to-station. It must be a death message! They were calling to tell Boyd first so he could tell me.

I dialed long distance for Altus. Virginia answered. "Sis," she said, "everything is better now. It's Daddy. He had another heart attack. If I had got you a few hours ago I would have told you to come quick because we thought he was going. We've taken him to the hospital and he seems to be better now. But you'd better plan to come anytime."

"Have you called David?" I asked. David, our brother was a medical doctor in Memphis. He was two years younger than I.

"Yes," said Virginia, "and the doctor is going to call him later today and tell him how Dad is."

I felt better at once. If David were not on his way to Altus, things were not too bad. Virginia, five years my junior, was the youngest of the family. We loved her dearly and usually did her bidding. I wondered if I were someone else when I found myself saying, "We can't come today. Boyd is out of town with some of the other faculty members. But I can get in touch with him, and you let me know if there is any change." She said she would, and I knew she was crying when we hung up.

Billy, our ten-year-old, came in from school. "Hi, Mom," he said, and started to tell me something.

When I shushed him, all three children looked at me as though I had called a strike on their favorite batter. So I tried to explain. "Look, children," I said. "Grandfather Moore is very sick and I am trying to decide what to do. Please run and play or do your homework while Mother thinks."

"Are we going to go to Altus?" asked Billy.

"Is Grandfather going to die?" asked Anne.

"MIND ME!" I said, wishing I would act like a Christian in

front of them. They walked slowly to their rooms. I could hear them talking softly to one another.

Are we going to Altus? Is Grandfather going to die? I tried to focus my mind on something I was not used to—one very dear to me was seriously ill.

Daddy had a heart condition. We all knew that. Recently he had traveled to Memphis to go through David's new clinic. How proud he was of his only son! David found that Daddy had a tired heart but that it should be all right for five to fifteen years.

Daddy was seventy-four. His age was strictly hush-hush, however. He was almost fifteen years older than mother and always felt he would never live to see his children grown. Now we all were married, and our Elizabeth, one of his seven grandchildren, was almost as tall as he.

He had retired several years ago, broken up his corporation, and about ten days later started a new business—this time wholesale groceries. In a few years it grew so large that he was forced to either sell out or get someone to help. So Virginia and Larry, her husband, moved down from Chicago.

Although Chicago was home to Larry, he was intrigued by the thought of an independent business. And since Virginia was taken by the thought of being home again, they had come. Virginia found she missed Chicago and their friends there far more than she had imagined, but Larry took to the business like a first love. There was no doubt about their staying. And it meant a lot to us to see how Larry felt. We knew everything was not easy.

Daddy was an individualist. And in spite of the fact that we did not mention it, we all knew age had not mellowed his patience. Nor had he ever been a spendthrift, with one exception: his children's education. We three had all the education we wanted and without one cent of expense to ourselves—piano lessons from the most expensive teacher in the college, concerts, medical school. That was his dream for his children, and he made his dream come true.

Daddy was a deacon in the Altus First Baptist Church. He did not make much of his position, but his Lord and his church were the foundation of his life. He did not talk about his faith, but he breathed it. Daddy was a deacon like he was a father. He worked, he paid the bills, he loved us. He worshiped God and delighted in his good, green earth; he frequented God's house and kept his day holy. We felt, rather than heard, the stuff of which Daddy was really made.

Now, for the first time in the almost forty years he lived in Altus, he was in the hospital. I ought to go, I told myself. I ought to leave right now.

But if I went, I would have to call Boyd, and that was what I did not want to do. We had moved to Fort Worth only recently. The past six years, my husband had been pastor of Houston's First Baptist Church. Now, back at Southwestern Seminary where he was head of the department of systematic theology, for the first time he was "out with the boys," his colleagues in teaching, on a fishing trip. I wanted him to have that fishing trip. And I knew that if I called him to say Virginia thought we should come, he would say, "Then we'd better go." So I waited.

The heavy feeling in my heart, however, would not leave. I found myself making plans to leave even though I kept saying I would not have to go. Virginia would call and say Daddy was better, and it would be a good thing for me to stay home. When finally all three children were fed, bathed, kissed, and tucked in bed, I began to wonder why Virginia had not called.

I dialed long distance and asked for Mother's number. There was no answer. I tried the Andersons. Larry answered the phone. He told the operator that Mother and Virginia were at the hospital and gave that number.

Virginia answered the call at the hospital. She did not sound like herself. She told me Daddy was very sick, awfully sick. Was David on the way? No, they had not called him yet.

Just then, Mother took the phone. Daddy was indeed very sick, she told me, but everything was all right. There was nothing I could do right now, and she would rather I waited to come until the doctor called David. David's best connection might be to fly to Fort Worth so that he could come from there with us.

Mother's voice was calm. I wondered at her strength and marveled that even at a time like this she was the one we leaned on. I told her I would be ready to do whatever she asked. I tried to tell her I was loving her and Daddy and thinking of them. She seemed to understand exactly what I meant. I hung up with much of my confusion lifted.

Now I knew I should call Boyd. I could explain to him how things were so he would know what to expect.

Boyd did not seem to need an explanation. He understood. "I think we should go," he said. "As soon as you find out about David, call me, and someone will take me to the Jacksboro highway and you can pick me up on the way."

Sometime in the early hours after midnight, David flew in from Memphis. I fixed the back of the car so the children could sleep, and David and I sped down the Jacksboro highway. Ralph Phelps and Jesse Northcutt took Boyd to the highway. We tried to thank them, but they acted as though it were nothing at all to spend half the night on the bumpy back roads to and from the fishing site.

I told Boyd and David all I knew about Daddy's condition.

"It sounds terminal," said David.

It was morning when we arrived in Altus. How strange it was to drive pass Moore's O. G. & S. Wholesale Groceries and the house on Live Oak Street and on to the hospital.

Daddy was awake and lucid when we walked into the room. "Hello, son," he said, "and Connie and Boyd." We embraced him and Mother and Virginia and Larry. We told Daddy he looked fine and asked him why he was in the hospital trying to scare us? All of us stood around the bed talking to him. He looked at us and said, "Now this is what I call doing things decently and in order."

We laughed and the tension was lifted. Daddy looked grey, but I felt sure he was over the worst and would soon be his usual self. I think I was the only one who did not know the truth. David knew, of course. Mother and Larry and Virginia were with Daddy so constantly they could tell what was happening. Boyd had been with the dying too often not to recognize death when he saw it.

I decided we should be practical and efficient about the whole thing. Someone needed to be at home with the children all the time, and we wanted one of us with Daddy all the time. I made a schedule so we all could help at the hospital. David and mother insisted on staying there constantly. The rest of us would come and go by a schedule.

Daddy loved David's care and Mother's presence. But not even our most loving and efficient care changed the grey look. Soon Daddy thought he was back in the warehouse. One corner of the hospital room especially bothered him. "Now there's plenty of room over there," he said. "You boys help me stack those hundred-pound sacks of sugar over there."

"Yes, sir," said David, moving a table and some flowers there.

Daddy kept looking around for more space. "We don't want to waste anything," he said. Finally, there were flowers everywhere. "That's better," said Daddy.

One night he said nothing at all. The intravenous feeding ran steadily through the tube into his arm. It was my time to be with him, so Mother and David had left for a moment. His forehead was so hot, I sponged it gently with a damp cloth. I softly kissed his wrinkled cheek. There was no response to my touch; his heavy, uneven breathing went on just as before. And then I knew that Daddy was dying.

My silent tears fell on his shiny bald head. Music from some old memory flooded my mind. Was it "Amazing Grace"? Daddy loved to try to sing it at church, or whistle its melody while he trained the vines on the backyard fence. I realized at that moment that he and Mother were the reasons my life had been joy and music. It seemed the whole room was filled with pink Altus National Bank checks, checks signed "J. M. Moore" that had paid for my piano lessons, my illnesses, my Christmas dolls, my college education, my Easter hat, my Sunday shoes.

1

O Day of Rest and Gladness

Daddy was whistling a high, clear tune out in the backyard when I opened my eyes to sun pouring through the bedroom window. That meant it was Sunday. And that meant the *Daily Oklahoman* was here and I could look at the funny papers. I jumped out of bed into the shivery cold and raced to the dining room beside the stove where it was warmest. I could hear Mother in the kitchen. The smell of fresh biscuits drew me into her presence.

"Good morning, Connie Betty," she said. "I'm glad you're up. Be very careful when you put on your stockings. I want this pair to last longer than the others." The other pair came to a tragic end when I had run through the Junior department in the basement of the church and hit the hard cement on all fours.

I went back to the dining room and began to dress. Mother had laid all our clothes in neat stacks on the dining room table. I reached for my long underwear and began pulling it on. It was fresh, clean, and stayed close to my body. I liked having it fit so tightly. Today I would not have to fold over the legs when I pulled my stockings on. They would fit over the underwear smoothly, and only a slight ridge at my ankle would reveal its presence.

I picked up my supporters and drew them over my shoulders.

They dangled down waiting to be hitched to my stockings. I picked up the new pair of silk ribbed Sunday stockings. They were a bright, shiny tan—oh, so beautiful! I pulled them on carefully over the underwear. I was a big girl now, almost nine, and did not need any help from Mother, even on Sundays. Once I got the stockings over the place above my ankle where the underwear began, it was easy going. I hitched them tautly to the supporters and walked around the room looking at them before I put on my Sunday black sateen bloomers.

I pulled the bloomers up until the elastic around the legs was just below my supporters. I knew Mother would make me pull them down to my knees before we left for Sunday school, but I enjoyed my liberty a few moments.

I sat on the floor and put on my black patent leather Roman sandals. I used the button hook to get them buttoned although they were not so new as to need it any more. I had worn them since September, and February would soon be over. In March I would get a pair of summer Sunday shoes. They would probably be white slippers, which I would like, but not as much as I liked Roman sandals. I finished buttoning them and began to dance around the room to feel their softness.

"Breakfast!" called Mother. I grabbed my starched Sunday underskirt and pulled it over my head. The last thing in my stack was the dress I had worn yesterday. We children were not allowed to put on our outside Sunday clothes until after breakfast.

Mother opened the back door and called, "Marvin, breakfast is ready. If we don't eat right away, we won't get to Sunday school on time." Then she began spooning out the oatmeal.

Daddy scraped his shoes on the back porch step and came in. He was not hurrying. On Sunday nothing could hurry Daddy. Sunday was a day of rest, and Daddy rested by slowing his pace. "Why there's my big girl," said Daddy in a proud voice, "all up and dressed." He did not even notice my bloomers.

Mother noticed them the minute I walked into the kitchen. "Pull your bloomers down to the proper place, Connie Betty," she said.

Mother always noticed my bloomers—ever since the day I brought home the picture of my first grade class. The day it was to be taken Mother sent me to school in my blue linen dress she had embroidered in pink flowers. It was rather short so the matching blue linen bloomers would show just the leg bands which also were embroidered with pink flowers. Before I got to school, I pulled the bloomer legs high. When we were lined up for the picture, I was put on the front row because I was one of the shorter class members. Just before the camera clicked, one of my bloomer legs fell down.

Mother cut off the bottom part of the picture, so when anyone saw it at our house, they got only the best impression. But the other mothers of children in the class were not so thoughtful. Mother did not think it was funny—not for years and years.

So I pulled down my bloomer legs and got into my place at the kitchen table. We bowed our heads, and Daddy returned thanks. After he said, "Amen," he leaned over and kissed Mother's cheek. I do not know how old I was before I realized that not all daddies thanked God for food and then kissed their wives at the table.

I hated oatmeal, but Mother had heard at P.T.A. that it was good for children, especially skinny children, so I had to eat it. After that, there were scrambled eggs and big, fluffy biscuits. When we pulled a biscuit apart, a little wisp of steam curled above the middle, and a big chunk of butter melted like lightning.

Daddy buttered several biscuits and put them on his plate. The butter ran out of them and trickled down in little yellow rivulets. When he finished the rest of his food, he knifed a large piece of butter and put it in the middle of his plate. Over it he poured white Karo syrup. He mashed and mixed it with a fork. It took him ages to get just the consistency he wanted. When he finished, it was the most beautiful honey-gold confection ever to grace a breakfast table. I held out my biscuit.

"Please, Daddy," I begged. "Let me have some too."

Daddy feigned astonished disgust. "Can't I ever eat my own

food?" he asked. He filled my biscuit until it dripped over the sides. The golden, gooey sweetmeat tasted so good. And I knew Daddy would make some more if I really wanted it.

"More, Daddy," I said.

The pleasant knowledge of being the center of my parents' attention was interrupted by the arrival in the kitchen of my pajama-clad, six-year-old brother. "Don't give her all of it," said David. Mother got him into his place at the table and dished out more oatmeal.

"I must get Virginia up and give her her breakfast," said Mother. "I don't see how time can fly so fast on Sunday morning. If we don't hurry we'll surely be late to Sunday school."

Mother hurried. Three-year-old Virginia was soon fed and dressed. Then Mother did the dishes while David and I argued over who had looked at which funny and why it took so long for anybody to look at one page.

Daddy sewed a new piece of adhesive tape to the inside of his toupee. Mother did not like the toupee, so she pretended not to see what he was doing so laboriously. With a show of dispatch, Daddy got out his typewriter and worked on his Sunday school lesson. Spread out around the table were his Sunday school quarterly, a huge old Bible, and his *Mother, Home and Heaven Book.* He read and thought and typed, read and thought and typed.

Daddy taught a class of boys in the Young People's department. He loved teaching Sunday school and took his work very seriously. When we had lived in Tennessee, he taught a class of men. Mother taught their wives. Once the classes held a contest to see which could draw the largest attendance. Daddy's class lost, so the men had to prepare a dinner for the ladies. For entertainment, the men mimicked the ladies. Daddy and Mother would laugh whenever they remembered the red-haired man who represented Mother. In the hall hung two large pictures of the classes. It was easy to find Daddy; he was standing in the front row of his class with his Bible under his arm. Mother had her arms around the ladies standing on both sides of her, and she looked very fashionable in her long-waisted, short-skirted dress.

Mother now worked in the Primary department of Altus First Church. David and I were both in this department, although I was due to graduate into the Junior department in October. I tried to get promoted the year before by having a lapse of memory about my age. The new rule about promotion was that a child nine years old by the first of April could go into the Junior department. All the children who fell in that age group were fitted into gorgeous, yellow crepe-paper costumes and marched up to the platform in the church auditorium to receive their diplomas. The longer I looked at the little sunbeams in their crepe-paper costumes, the more confused I became about my birthday. I told my teacher I was sure my birthday was very close to April, and in short order I was being fitted into a delectable, swishy cape and hat.

How Mother could have seen me so quickly among all those identical, excited creatures swathed in yellow crepe-paper, I do not know. But suddenly she seemed to be towering over me, her eyes looking straight into mine. "Connie Betty Moore," she said in *that* voice, "you know very good and well your birthday is in May. Now go right back to your class where you belong."

I was scared, but there was also a satisfaction about the whole thing. I had worn the crepe-paper costume. Everyone in my class was green with envy. I told them all about it.

Mother called David and me away from the funnies long enough to get us into our Sunday clothes. I was wearing last year's Sunday winter dress, but nothing in town could touch it for glamour. It was black satin, accordion pleated all over. Mother sent it to the cleaners to get the pleats put in and made it especially to go with the hat.

The hat was one an enterprising store manager had me to model in a program at the Lion's Club. Daddy was there, and people told him they never saw me look so pretty. Daddy bought the hat on the spot even though it cost five dollars. Mother was aghast with unbelief. Even she rarely paid that much for hats, for Daddy would have called it wasteful.

Mother straightened the pink crepe de Chine brim of my hat

and smoothed the black velvet ribbons down my back. "Now quick," she ordered, "all of you children get in the car. Connie, help Virginia. And don't shove her in—lift her up on the fender. But be careful. Where is David?" she asked, looking around.

"I'm in here," came David's voice from the room farthrest back in the house.

"Oh, no!" Mother wailed. "Now we will be late."

"Well, Mother," I reminded, "you said he should have good health habits every day."

"Connie BETTY!" She rushed toward the most distinctive room in our house. It was made from parts of an old frame building that once housed the First Baptist Church. No one had wanted the old building. So when Daddy finally offered to buy it, his brother deacons praised him for his generosity to the Lord's cause.

It irritated them no end, however, when Daddy's sacrificial gift turned out to be a material blessing for him. He towed the old building away and converted it into a small rent house. Parts of it he used on our present house. He reasoned sensibly that one room in the house needed opaque windows. Since he now found himself in possession of such, he used them and saved money by not having to buy shades. Ours was the only house in Altus with stained glass windows in the bathroom.

Daddy swished his paper out of the typewriter. "Where are the car keys, Mother?" he called.

"I'll get them," Mother called back. "You and the girls go on to the car."

Daddy walked to the car with us. He stopped to examine the peach trees beside the house and said, "This is a beautiful morning."

Mother came scurrying out of the house holding the car keys in one hand and pulling David along with the other. Daddy cranked the car, and it sputtered and chugged.

Daddy leisurely backed the car out of the driveway. He took off his hat and said how-do-you-do to a neighbor who chanced to come out of her front door.

"Hurry just a little, Marvin," said Mother. "We have only seven minutes until the first bell rings."

"It won't take us two minutes longer if we go slow and enjoy the ride," said Daddy. He continued driving not one whit faster all the way to church. Mother had us out of the car almost before he pulled the hand brake. We got inside the church door just as the bell began to ring.

After Sunday school, Mother herded us into the church auditorium for the preaching service. We met Daddy at the back. He led the way down the aisle to the fifth row from the front, center. He stopped to talk in a loud stage whisper to any friend he saw nearby while Mother and we three children took our places in the pew. Daddy sat next to the aisle, handed his hat over to Mother, smoothed the edges of his toupee, cleared his throat once or twice, and took out his watch to check the time.

The singing part of the service was my favorite. We had a good singer, and no one could resist following him when he asked us to "sing it heartily." Daddy sang off key, but he sang off key with all his heart. Especially on "Amazing Grace" his off key would sound out above all the rest. I listened to him singing so heartily, and I thought how nice it would be for him when he got to heaven. In that perfect place, he could sing on key and have real hair growing on his head. I was sure that was all it would take to make my Daddy completely happy.

One of the other deacons came to our pew and leaned over to ask Daddy if he would help pass the offering plates. He was soon going along the aisles gathering the offerings. We liked to see Daddy take the offering. When David asked him what they did with the money in the plates, he said, "The preacher gets it." I supposed the preacher must have an altar in his office where he burned the money as a sweet sacrifice unto the Lord.

Suddenly, a lady behind us gave a little scream and people around her gasped. I turned in time to see Daddy righting the collection plate which he had just pretended to dump into her lap. It was empty all the time.

Daddy was soon back in his place at the end of the row. He

cleared his throat loudly, folded his arms over his chest, and for the rest of the service lived the part of a veritable pillar of the church. He was not the only deacon who acted up during collection taking. Once while Daddy sat in the pew, another deacon gathering the offering lifted off Daddy's toupee and put it in the plate. Pretty soon after that, Daddy stopped wearing the toupee.

During the sermon, Mother and Daddy drank in the Word of God preached to them by a pastor they loved and respected. Brother Burton was saying something about the righteous shining like the stars forever and ever. I heard some of it, but mostly I wiggled. Pauline and her parents were sitting next to us. She was in the Junior department, but she was still allowed to have a pencil and paper in church. Mother had tried that with us for awhile, but we were always dropping the pencil. It usually rolled all the way to the pulpit, so we were restricted to handkerchiefs.

Handkerchiefs, we discovered, made no sound when they were dropped, and they stayed where they fell. We learned to have a lovely time with them. You could fold them across with the corners matching and make a diaper. Two fingers made a pretend doll, and with time and patience, one hand could put the diaper on the other one. Or you could roll up two corners until they came together in the middle. This made two people in a hammock, and we would carefully pick up the other two corners and swing the "people" to and fro. When we tired of swinging them, we gave the handkerchief a snap and the people rolled out. It was not the most exciting pastime in the world, but it had to do.

Being in church on Sunday was as much a part of our lives as breathing, and we learned early to take it quietly. I learned the hard way when I was two. Nurseries were unheard of, and I had been coming to church since I was six weeks old. As a two-year-old, I was expected to stay within a restricted zone either immediately in front of, or on the seat between, my parents. About the middle of the sermon, I decided to climb over the seat to visit with some engaging people who were smiling at me from the pew behind. Nor was I dissuaded by Mother's gentle tugs on my pink ruffled dress. When Daddy finally sat me firmly in our pew, I began to howl.

Daddy picked me up and carried the commotion out of church. He broke a small switch off a tree and used it on my legs. I screamed loud enough for the whole church to hear. People glowered at Daddy as he carried me on his arm, snubbing and sniffing but quite subdued, back to his place beside Mother. Mother had not changed her expression during the whole episode but looked straight at the preacher as though nothing had happened. She trusted Daddy implicitly, even with me.

I snuggled down in Daddy's arms and went to sleep. That almost broke his heart, Mother said. I rarely went to sleep in the daytime, and he wondered if he had possibly hurt me. When the service was over, I woke to be petted and loved. While Mother fixed dinner, Daddy sliced a juicy, cool apple and fed me its thinly scraped innards from the edge of a table knife.

But I had learned about church. I cannot remember if David and Virginia had similar experiences. We all knew how far we could go. We often went that far, but it was hardly worthwhile to go farther.

This bright morning the service did not seem long. We were soon standing to sing the invitation. At the beginning of the second verse of "Just as I Am," Pauline edged over to me. "When are you going to join the church?" she asked.

"I don't know," I whispered back.

"You ought to do it this morning like Brother Burton said," she replied. "You might die and go to hell before you have another chance."

I did not answer her. I was furious. The *idea* of her telling me when I ought to join the church! Maybe my parents could tell me, but no one else. And I had been taught better theology than to worry about going to hell because I had not joined the church. She and I both knew that joining the church had nothing to do with it; it was trusting Jesus in your heart that kept you out of hell. And I did trust Jesus. *I trust Jesus,* I silently reassured myself. After the benediction, I went out the aisle away from

Pauline. My stomach felt strange, and I wanted to get outside.

Outside was clear blue sky and warm sun that come once every February in Oklahoma. I swung my coat over my arm and ran to the car.

Daddy and David were already beside the car. David climbed into it while Daddy looked back impatiently to the church for Mother. Mother spoke to everyone and everyone had a smile for her. She shook hands with Brother Burton saying, "The sermon was such a blessing." Mother said it almost every Sunday, and she felt it more deeply every time she said it. She took Virginia's hand and started for the car.

"Holt and Bertha will be wondering what happened to us." said Daddy as he turned the car south from the church. We were going to Eldorado, a small town about thirty miles southwest of Altus, to have Sunday dinner with Daddy's brothers Holt and Henry Moore and their families. Since there were two families of them, we went there twice as often as they came to see us. It was an unusual Sunday when the families were not together one place or the other. Today Aunt Bertha was preparing the dinner, and my stomach growled with anticipation. There would be great platters filled with golden hunks of fried chicken, fluffy potatoes with creamed chicken gravy to go over them, plate after plate of steaming hot biscuits, mounds of home-made country butter, sweet potatoes with marshmallows on top, dozens of deviled eggs, angel food cake, and we could hope for a freezer of ice cream. I hoped. I hoped hard.

We headed out the sandy road toward the Salt Fork of Red River. Old Salt Fork was a mean, unpredictable river. When a rain came, the river might stay under the bridge, or it might cut a new course a mile away and a mile wide, roaring along in red fury. But it had not rained in a long time this year, and only pools of calm water stood under the wooden bridge as we started across. Mother always prayed that no one would be coming from the other direction. Passing on the bridge could be done, but it was a tight squeeze and Daddy did not like to slow down for it. Mother's prayers were usually granted, and today we crossed it alone to the deafening clatter of its wooden planks under the wheels.

"This is a fine bridge," shouted Daddy. "You children take a good look at it. See that curve in it? That's so it will bend with the current of the water when she gets up high. And it never has washed away yet."

We always took a good look at it and marveled that it had not washed away. It never did wash away, either. The river simply plowed out a new course a mile or so away, and the old bridge was finally torn down.

Between the river and Olustee, a tiny village between Altus and Eldorado, were five miles of deep sand and "the hill." As warm and dry as it was today, we were almost sure to have to push the car up the hill. Mother already had us out of our Sunday clothes and into something better for playing with our cousins in Eldorado. We were sure to be allowed out of the car to climb the hill while Daddy and Mother got the car over it.

Daddy drove the car as hard as he could when we neared the hill, and we almost made it to the top. We strained forward in our seats and tried to will the car on as it went slower and slower and finally chugged to a stop near the top. Steam curled up from the radiator as Daddy pulled the hand brake, jumped from the car, and put a board under the left back tire. The board stopped us from rolling, and Daddy ordered us children out. With Mother calling to us to be careful and not go farther than the foot of the hill, we gleefully left them to the task at hand. Mother took the wheel.

"Now, Mother," said Daddy, "you just give her all she's got and keep her straight in the road, and I'll do the rest."

Mother did and Daddy did the rest. The car moved a few inches forward and came back a foot. Daddy would dig out sand from in front of the wheels, he and Mother got the car up that far, and Daddy put the board under the back wheel again. Finally with a great roar, the balance of power shifted to the down side instead of the up side. At that point, Mother moved over, Daddy grabbed the door, took the wheel, and they rode triumphantly down. At the foot of the hill, the car was stopped. While Mother fanned herself and called us to get in the car, Daddy inspected the radiator. "She's going to make it all right," he announced. "She'll cool off as we go along."

After that, it was smooth sailing. There was no bridge at all over Boggy Creek, but there was no water either. One Thanksgiving there had been so much water in old Boggy that Daddy had to test its depth before taking the car across. He rolled his pants up above his knees and waded barefoot into the swirling creek. On the other side, he motioned Mother to come, and she drove the car safely through the water to the other side. Today we merely dipped down and up and were soon passing the gypsum mills just outside of Eldorado. In less than an hour and a half from the time we left the church, we were storming Aunt Bertha's fragrant kitchen, everyone was laughing and talking at the same time, and David and I were trying to push each other off the stool of the player piano.

You cannot possibly know how Aunt Bertha's cooking can fill you, unless you have eaten one of her meals. We went away from the table, all twelve of us, rubbing our tummies and moaning contentedly. While the ladies washed and put away the huge stack of dishes, the men stretched out in overstuffed chairs talking politics or telling yarns.

Later, the men went down to Uncle Holt and Henry's drugstore or out to the farm to see how the wheat was coming along. If they went to the drugstore, David and I always pestered to go along. Daddy usually let us. What fun it was! We were almost sure to get a grape soda or an ice cream cone, or even an Eskimo pie. We took the goody over to one of the little round tables with its dainty, twisted iron legs. We sat in one of the four matching chairs and felt we were in the lap of luxury.

Then we looked at magazines. There seemed to be thousands of them. David and I were not allowed to have the new ones, but those with the covers torn off were ours to do with as we liked. One magazine had a page of paper dolls. It was my favorite. David liked the ones with men bulging their muscles.

One afternoon I found a magazine with sad, sad stories in it about ladies whose husbands had left them. When I told Mother about it in my most mournful tones, she looked at Daddy. "Marvin," she said, "I don't believe you pay a bit of attention to those children in that store." After that, we did not always have a free hand in the magazine section, but even so we never got to the end of the supply.

In the back of the drug store was a domino parlor. We were absolutely forbidden to enter it, but one time I went to the door and peeked in. It did not look at all like a parlor. It was filled with men, laughing and smoking and arguing with one another as they played dominoes on small tables. Daddy did not go in; he completely ignored the place. Uncle Holt went back and forth taking Cokes and ice cream. He frowned as he went about his work. Uncle Henry was the mainstay of the domino parlor. "There's not a thing wrong with it," he insisted, "and we make more money back there in a day than we do at the front in two."

Since Daddy himself played dominoes at home, he did not argue with them about the parlor. He did try to talk them into closing the store on Sunday, however. "You need a day of rest," he said. "Why, I wouldn't open my business on Sunday for anything in the world. And I believe I make just as much in six days as I would in seven. The Lord knew what he was doing when he told us to rest one day out of seven."

At Aunt Bertha's house, the ladies finished the dishes and went upstairs to rest. They loosened their corsets, took off their shoes, and lay on the bed talking. They always started talking about how the children were growing and getting prettier or handsomer every day. Then one of them would begin on a particular problem she was having with her child, or she would complain mildly about something her husband would or would not do. The other ladies listened patiently, making sympathetic sounds under their breath, and immediately took up for the one under fire. "But he's so good natured," Mother said to Aunt Bertha. "But Marvin works so hard," Aunt Bertha said to Mother. It was an unwritten law that only a mother or wife could complain about her own; if anyone agreed with her, no one would have any fun. As it was, all the ladies got to air their woes, received assurance that their troubles were nothing in comparison, and then felt smug since, after all, no family compared to hers.

We always left for home about four-thirty or five o'clock in order to get back to B.Y.P.U. by six forty-five. At the preaching service, our singer Mr. Huber and his wife sang a duet. I loved to hear them, and something always felt warm inside me to see him with his arm around her as they stood singing.

Brother Burton preached on prayer. " 'The effectual fervent prayer of a righteous man availeth much,' " he quoted over and over. "God wants us to care about what we ask him. If we really care, we will be fervent." I think he was talking about winning souls to Christ, but I was so sleepy, I cannot be sure.

David and Virginia, soundly sleeping, were carried out after the service. I held on to Mother's hand and crept sleepily to the car. By the time the two younger children were put to bed, I was wide awake.

I took my time getting ready for bed. A wind had come up from the north, and it was cold again. The featherbed would feel good. Mother let me say "Now I lay me down to sleep" beside her in the warm room before I went into the unheated bedroom.

After she tucked me in, it occurred to me that I had not said "Now I lay me" very fervently. I tried to repeat it fervently, but I was not satisfied. What did I really care about, I asked myself? There must be something I really, really wanted. There was. There was something I wanted to be. I wanted, really wanted, to be as beautiful and sweet as Snow White, whom I read about in my fairy storybook.

"Dear God," I prayed fervently, "please grant that in the morning when I wake up I will have cheeks as white as snow, lips as red as blood, and long curls hanging down my back as black as the ebony wood of the window pane."

I closed my eyes. Sunday was over. I dimly heard the reassuring sound of a parent passing by in the hall. "Good night, Daughter," said Daddy.

2

To the Work,

to the Work!

Monday morning I awoke when Daddy slammed the door of the pickup truck and roared off to work. It was still dark. He did not slam it in anger, but because he was in a hurry. There was work to be done, and on work days, nothing could slow Daddy down. To him, being late to the office was a cardinal vice.

During the fourth, fifth, and sixth years of my life, Daddy was office manager of a wholesale grocery business in Cookeville, Tennessee. Only five miles away in Algood lived Uncle Doc and Uncle Fred, Daddy's brothers, and their families. One icy morning, after spending Christmas with them, we started home in plenty of time for Daddy to arrive at the office. He started getting us off in plenty of time, that is, except the time it took to load all the toys Santa brought plus the five of us into the coupé. When we were finally on the way, Daddy tried to make up time by going faster than usual.

"Marvin, slow down!" Mother said as we rounded a frozen curve.

"Now, Alva," Daddy replied, "I'd hate to be late to the office after a holiday."

Those words were quoted by his brothers in good-natured ridicule many times afterwards, because at that moment the car began to skid into a ditch. The car eased over on its side exactly between two posts of a wire fence. There was much talk later about what might have happened if we had landed on a post. Mother always said we could thank the good Lord for sparing our lives and try to dedicate them to God more wholly. Daddy rubbed the top of his head during such discussions, and said nothing at all.

Mother told Uncle Doc that Daddy's face was as white as the snow on the ground as he managed to open the door on his side of the car and lift us out one by one. The thing I remember most about the accident is that it was a dreadfully cold morning, and it seemed an age before somebody came along to pick us up and take us into Cookeville. Apparently, no one else was trying to get to an office so early.

But even this haste-makes-waste episode failed to change Daddy's ways. He always hurried to his place of business. He loved his work. It was his hobby as well as his vocation. He worked early and late, six days a week. And all he asked from it was the chance to make an honest living and to get ahead enough to educate his children well.

His beloved, native Tennessee hills had not given him this chance. There were too many sons to provide for in Daddy's home for him to hope for a saddle horse and a piece of land when he grew up. But he meant to have them. He decided to go west to the land of opportunity and not to return until he had gold pieces to jingle in his pockets.

Daddy's elder brother, Dr. J. T. Moore, Sr., describes in his memoirs, *Dr. Tom*, how Daddy, then a teen-age lad, gave his old coon dog Tige to "the Milligan boys" to keep while he was away. "I can see Marvin with his sentimental, tender heart, with tears in his eyes, brushing old Tige, not expecting to ever see him again, turning and walking sadly away, crossing two rail fences along the path through the green fields over which we had traveled so many times. . . . My five brothers made prosperous business men. Marvin drifted for awhile, but married and settled down in Oklahoma and was perhaps the best and most successful."

Whatever Daddy did at his place of business never entered my childhood thoughts. All daddies worked. And sometimes they worried about their work. Whenever Daddy was cross, Mother said, "Daddy is worried about business." She said it as if that explained everything and we could be sure Daddy would take care of whatever problem arose.

I understood more about Daddy's work during my teen-age years. Then the depression was at its height—or depth, I should say. Daddy displayed the Blue Eagle of the NRA on his office window. Some people counted the eagle's wings or feet or something, and they said it was the mark of the beast prophecied in Revelation, but I do not think Daddy ever saw it that way. He was solid Democrat and never voted any other way except once when the Democratic candidate was a Catholic. On the inside of Daddy's office, over the Blue Eagle, was a big, white streamer printed in bright red letters, SAVE OUR CONSTITUTION.

One night I waked to strange sounds. Was Daddy making those groanings? He was indeed. He was pacing up and down, up and down, in his and Mother's room, and often a moan escaped his lips. I heard Mother's soft reassuring voice. Daddy stopped his pacing and they talked awhile. I feel sure I heard them praying together as I drifted back to sleep.

"What was the matter with Daddy last night?" I asked Mother the next morning.

"Just business, darling. Daddy is worried about some hides he needs to sell."

"Hides," I said in disgust and wrinkled my nose to show my feelings. Daddy bought hides as a side line to his regular business of feed and seed. He salted the hides himself in a special warehouse. Whenever he came home after a salting, he took a hot, soapy bath and put on fresh clothes. He hung his hide-salting clothes in the back yard and washed them with the hose before Mother put them in the regular wash. But the hide smell stayed everywhere for hours.

"Don't you turn up your nose, young lady!" said Mother sharply. "Those hides may very well send you to college some day. You'd better be thankful to have a daddy who is willing to do an honest day's work for his family. You just better remember that you don't come from any proud, wealthy people who had money handed them on a silver platter. You come from people who had to work and who've been glad to work for what they got. Don't you ever look down on any honest work or anybody who does it. Work is an honorable thing and don't you forget it!"

"Yes, ma'am," I said meekly. Anyone with a grain of sense in her head said yes, ma'am, meekly when Mother talked like that. I knew very well she wished Daddy would stop buying hides; I had heard her say so many times. But it was not because of the smell—I knew that too.

"It's just that you don't need to do that kind of work anymore, Marvin," I heard her tell Daddy not just once. "You have more than enough to do as it is."

On this particular day, Daddy put through a call to Houston. Somebody there wanted the warehouse full of hides. With great rejoicing Daddy sold them all. I know he did not lose a penny, and I would be very surprised if he did not make a few. But the depression stopped his hide buying.

Times stayed tense for Daddy at the office. It was hard for him to relax when he got home. One noon he came in for a quick meal. We all bowed our heads for Daddy to give thanks, and he began in his hearty, telephone-answering voice, "Oklahoma Grain and Seed Company!" We burst out laughing, and Daddy smiled, heaved a sigh, and started again, "Dear Lord, we thank thee for this food . . ." while Mother slipped her hand into his big rough one.

After I learned to use a typewriter, I supposedly helped Daddy in the office at times during the summer. I loved to watch the farmers pull up to the big elevator scales with their loads of golden wheat.

"What are you paying today, Mr. Moore?" they called out.

"We're paying top prices on the Chicago market," Daddy replied, "seventeen cents a bushel."

"Seventeen cents!" The farmer exclaimed. "Why I thought everybody in town was paying eighteen."

"Oh Lordy, no!" Daddy half groaned rubbing his hand over his bald head. I made a mental note to tell Mother that Daddy was taking the Lord's name in vain.

Daddy and the farmer haggled for awhile, and I could see the back of the wagon bed lifted off and the grain sliding down into the elevator. Daddy came into the office looking pleased. "Pay him seventeen and a quarter cents," he told the bookkeeper.

Later I heard him talking to someone in Chicago. "Well, Mr. Smith," he said, "I have you a couple of carloads of the finest wheat you ever saw." There was a pause. "Oh, I can sell it to you for nineteen cents," he used the friendliest tone you can imagine. "No, I can't sell it to you for eighteen," he was yelling now. "It cost me eighteen right here in Altus."

There was another pause. "Well I just can't do it for that." *Wham!* Down went the receiver into the phone hook. *Bang!* Out the door went Daddy. Pity the poor farmer who drove up next.

After awhile, the bookkeeper called Daddy to the phone. "It's long distance, Mr. Moore," he called.

Daddy came at a quick clip. *Bang!* went the door. "All right!" he yelled into the phone. "This is J. M. Moore. What can I do for you?"

After a silence during which neither the bookkeeper nor I even breathed, Daddy said softly into the phone, "I just can't sell it for eighteen and a half, Mr. Smith, but I'll tell you what I'll do. I'll make it to you for eighteen and three quarters if you want three carloads." The whole world seemed to stand still a moment.

Then Daddy smiled. "A-a-all right, Mr. Smith," he said cordially. "We'll get them there right away." He dropped the receiver into the hook and turned to the bookkeeper. "Call the Frisco and tell them we've got to have three cars on this siding tomorrow morning—well, hello there, John!" he called out to a farmer driving up on the elevator scales. The door closed after him with a friendly bang. He ran his hand through the wheat.

"What are you paying today, J. M.?" the farmer asked Daddy.

"Top Chicago prices—seventeen cents," he answered.

"Seventeen cents! Why, everybody in town is paying eighteen."

"Oh Lordy no!" said Daddy rubbing his head.

The first time Daddy came in the office while the bookkeeper was out on an errand, I confronted him with some statistics. "How can you tell a man in Chicago that wheat cost you eighteen cents a bushel," I asked defiantly, "when you know very good and well you only paid seventeen and a quarter?"

Daddy and I never could discuss a point in question without glaring at each other and raising our voices.

"Maybe you'd like to tell me, young lady, how much it cost to put that wheat into that elevator and then load it into those boxcars." Without waiting for my unlikely answer, he was outside again, shoveling wheat faster and more furiously than any of the men he had hired for the purpose.

The crises of the depression came to Altus when the banks started closing. This happened all across the country, of course, and with news of each closing came something close to panic. People made a run on the banks to draw out their money. Each day the banks' opening their doors in Altus was almost a miracle.

One morning, only the Altus National was open. All over town, people who had not got their money before the doors closed lost much or everything they possessed. For many, it meant their children would not have college educations. For others, it meant poverty-stricken old age, bills that could not be paid, and a lifetime of hard-come-by savings gone in a moment.

The lines started forming in front of Altus National. The run on it had begun. Most of the people in line were those who, not having too much, desperately needed that little. The tellers were unhurried; the line went slowly.

At our house, the telephone was constantly in use. "What are you going to do, Mr. Moore? Are you going to pull out while there's still a chance? I'll do whatever you do."

Daddy walked the floor. He was perhaps not one of the largest depositors of the bank, but what he had was there—his business funds, the children's education accounts in our own names, Mother and Daddy's checking and savings accounts. These were his friends, people waiting to see what he would do and trusting him to do the right thing.

Daddy talked to his business partners. One of them especially he loved and respected. "Mr. Moore," he said, "that bank is as sound as can be. Its resources are solid. The only thing that can close it is people like you and me and others demanding cash on the barrel head for no purpose at all—no purpose at all—except to see if we can get it. Of course, there isn't enough cash on hand for that. No bank keeps that much cash."

Mother was convinced. She knew everybody in the bank and her heart went out to them. It was the day she usually made a deposit; so she went uptown, took her place in line, waited patiently, and made her deposit. I have always wondered if she was the only one in town who added to her bank account that day.

The next day the bank was still open, but the lines were longer. Reports told of other failures. Hope was faint and courage was failing. "What are you going to do, Mr. Moore?"

Daddy got word that the situation was indeed grave, but a plane was due in the afternoon with the cash that was needed. If he and others would stand pat . . . if the plane got there in time . . . if . . .

Daddy and others like him did stand and wait. The plane got there. The cash arrived in time. Perhaps there is much more to the story than that; perhaps it was not as close a call as it seemed. At any rate, the bank doors opened every day they were supposed to be open, and we were among the few fortunate families of the depression.

In fact, the events of the depression made us almost well-to-do. Daddy thought of insurance as an expensive risk, almost a gamble. He saved his money and laid it aside for rainy days and the inevitable expense of sending his children to college. So in the days when cash was the scarcest commodity, Daddy had it. There was not a great deal of it, but during the depression it did not take a great deal. We lived the way we always lived, getting only what Daddy and Mother felt was necessary and paying for it with money that had been saved ahead of time. During the depression, this was wealth indeed.

The depression was unknown in my childhood days. Grade school was a carefree existence, the teachers were absolute authorities, and Mother was president of the P.T.A. With Daddy off to work, Mother would soon get David and me up and ready for school, so I wiggled my toes in the warmth of the blankets for the last few minutes before the day began.

As I adjusted my pillow it occurred to me that I did not have long black curls hanging down my back. My hair felt as straight and short as ever, and I was sure it was still very blond. Probably I did not have lips as red as blood either, and freckles would keep my cheeks from being white as snow. I sighed. It must be that I was not "effectual" enough. I was sure I had been "fervent." Next time I would concentrate on being effectual. I decided to get up.

There was little excitement getting dressed for school. I lapped over the legs of my long underwear the best I could and pulled on long cotton stockings. Over them came high-topped shoes that had to be laced. I hated them—absolutely *hated* them. The soles were thick and the tops were a dark brown. All the other girls at school wore the same kind, so I could not say a thing. But I did not like them one infinitesimal bit.

It did not matter a whit to me that Daddy told us how happy he used to be as a boy in Tennessee to have any shoes to wear. According to him, when he, his sisters, or his brothers got a pair of new shoes, it was like having Christmas and a birthday all at once. He also told us he walked three miles to school through rain, snow, or any kind of weather.

He walked to a one-room school, he said, up on a hill not far from Caney Fork River. Any time Daddy talked about that school, his eyes twinkled as they did when he was enjoying himself, and nothing he said about the hardships could ever convince us that he did not have a wonderful time every minute.

We liked to hear him tell about what happened to bad boys. When some boy (Daddy never mentioned any name) had to have a licking, the teacher sent him outside to find a switch for his punishment. His classmates judged the boy by the size of the switch he brought in. A sissy brought in a small stick he found on the ground; from there the switches graduated the boys up to a real he-man who brought in a good sized part of the limb of a tree. That boy could really take it, and according to Daddy, he did.

I never saw a switch at Washington Ward School, but Miss Wilson, teacher of Third-A grade, needed none. Daddy told us Miss Wilson came from a fine, old Tennessee family, and she was an excellent teacher. Her multiplication tables ring in my ears to this day. We learned them all number by number up to 12 times 12 is 144.

Miss Wilson taught us many things. Like any good teacher I have ever known, she added something extra without dropping a jot or a tittle from required subjects. She taught the Eighteenth Amendment to the Constitution.

On the blackboard she drew a narrow, straight road, and leading off from it, she drew two wide, curving lines. The sure way to get off the straight road that led to happiness was to get on the wide road of drink.

I can never remember Miss Wilson telling us any tragic stories about drunkards. She told us the story of a hero. Her example was a fine, handsome young man. He promised his mother he would never take a drink of liquor. When he went away from home, some of his friends tried to make him take a drink. They held him down and tried to force it down his lips. He refused. They became angry, hit him and kicked him, but he never gave in. He kept his promise. Miss Wilson knew the young man. He was glad he kept his promise, and we were glad too. We knew he was on the right road, and we wanted to be like him. She convinced us, not once, but many times. It was as indelible as 12 times 12 is 144.

About the middle of the morning, the whole school had recess. When the big bell up in the tower clanged, the pianists began playing marches in their respective parts of the building.

We made two straight lines and marched in time to the music out of the building. The lines formed all the way down the broad sidewalk which ran the length of the playground and separated the girls' side from the boys' side. When everyone marched out, we stood erect and silent until the bell clanged once again. Then, with whoops of joy, the boys ran to their side of the playground, the girls to the other, and we were free for . . . was it thirty minutes?

Out on the sunshiny playground, it began to seem very warm. Where my stockings bagged around my knees, it was moist and hot. It really was warm enough, I convinced myself, to roll my stockings into socks. If it got cooler before I went home (and thinking of Mother's reaction to seeing me in a different motif, I felt sure it would cool off), I could change back again. I ran to the girls' rest room, unhitched my stockings, and carefully beginning at the top I rolled them down to my shoes. Then I hoisted up the legs of the thick underwear and tucked them, along with the dangling supporters, under the ample full-gathered legs of my bloomers. Their firm bands of elastic kept everything in place although my dress had a new flair. The roll of stockings made rather thick anklets, and I did not think them pretty. But, ah, now I could run twice as fast!

The bell called us into line again, and Miss Wilson "left-righted" us rhythmically back to class. We had no more than got to our desks when she called my name. "Connie Betty Moore," she said emphatically, "when your mother sent you to school today, she saw to it that you were properly dressed. I think you'd better stay that way. You may be excused."

I cannot remember that it shamed me tremendously to be so caught up. I had known all along that release was temporary. It was blissful while it lasted. The worst thing, and something I had not anticipated, was that the underwear had stretched beyond repair. When I made the fold, it was almost double around my ankle. Crime just did not pay at Washington Ward School.

I never got into any real trouble at school. I think I bothered the teachers—like the many times in music period when Mr.

Vandervort had us sing do-re-mi-fa-sol-la-ti-do and I sang each note a third higher. It sounded so much more interesting that way. When Mr. Vandervort walked slowly down the aisles listening while we sang, I lost my nerve and started singing with the rest of the class. That way, it took him several days to discover who was harmonizing.

Eventually, I got to sing in the school chorus, under the supervision of Miss Crutcher, the principal. Mr. Vandervort played the piano accompanist. Miss Crutcher did not direct us, she polished us.

"Make your voices like a whisper," she whispered. Our voices would soften to a breath of air.

"Now lightly, with a happy sound," she commanded, and we sang with joyous hearts.

Miss Crutcher's chorus won many a first prize in the county contests. Oh, but those county contests were thrilling! Even Daddy came to listen to the finals. Miss Crutcher spent hours and hours of practice getting us ready for them. When our turn came to go on the stage to sing, Miss Crutcher sat on the front row of the City Auditorium and just looked at us. We were the only chorus without an adult standing in front of us to direct. We always sang softer than any other chorus. And we never ever dared make a mistake. For years, Miss Crutcher's glee club took first place.

Every year Miss Crutcher presented an operetta. My last year in Washington School, she chose me to be Titania, the queen of the fairies. Mother spent hours making my costume. How many packages of crepe paper did it take? Mother cut it in row on row of pointed scallops. She ruffled the scallops on a cheesecloth foundation. Just below my waist, she put a hoop. The full-length fairy gown was bouffant in a way that dreams are made of.

Mother made a glittering crown out of pasteboard, and a scepter with a star on top. Then Mother did something that made me the most envied character in any operetta for years to come. She bought several yards of white crepe de Chine. She outlined the long, white length with a rope of silver tinsel retrieved from a box which held Christmas decorations. She fitted it carefully around my shoulders, and behold! I was a fairy queen indeed, with my airy, sparkling train floating behind in regal beauty.

Of course, there was method in Mother's "madness." The length of crepe de Chine was exactly the amount needed to make my recital dress. That spring, Mother cut and sewed it into a sleeveless, long-waisted dress. The short skirt was the same crepe de Chine in rows of ruffles.

Besides being my recital dress, it was the one I wore one enchanting evening to Wichita Falls, Texas, to hear Paderewski in a piano concert. I am still not sure whether I was more impressed with Paderewski or the wonderful paved highway which appeared the moment we crossed the Red River and hit Texas territory. There is no doubt whatsoever in my mind which impressed Daddy more. For days we heard about Texas' marvelous use of tax money to build highways.

Mother talked only of Paderewski. It was she who told us to keep on clapping our hands after the great artist finished his concert. "If we clap long enough, he will play his 'Minuet,'" she said. We clapped until our hands were red and tired. Paderewski played many encores.

"Keep clapping," said Mother.

At last the white haired master bent over the keyboard for one last number. In the hush that followed, he played the delicate, winsome "Minuet." How we clapped when he finished, with no urging at all! It was something to tell about at school the next day.

It was clearly understood that I was to come straight home after school, and no dillydallying. The one exception was on music days when I stopped to take my piano lesson. Mrs. Putman taught me piano from the third grade through high school. I was one of her many students. We plagued her, argued with her, resisted her teaching, hated her, loved her, gave her presents, gave her migraine headaches, and told stories about her. Marguerite said she did not have any hair. I looked ever afterward as closely as I dared, but I could never be sure whether

her dark tresses were a wig or the real thing. Mother found out about our doubt and threatened me for dear life if I even so much as mentioned it to anyone. She used the same tone of voice as when she threatened me about telling David and Virginia there was no Santa Claus. So I let that investigation go, and I am not sure to this day about Mrs. Putman's hair.

Mrs. Putman was the most progressive teacher in Jackson County when it came to two-piano work. For the "William Tell Overture" we had three girls (It couldn't have been four! Could it?) at each piano. Ooh, those practice sessions! Mrs. Putman went straight to bed after each one. We were horrible. When she said to play softly, we were so soft you could hardly hear a sound. When she said to play a little louder, neighbors looked out windows toward the sound. When she said to count, we yelled one-two-three-four and did not stay together. When she said go slowly, we dragged it; when she said to pick up the tempo, we tore through the pages faster than the Lone Ranger ever hi-hoed Silver away to the range.

But Mrs. Putman endured to the end somehow. Year after year, her spring recitals were the ones at which no one forgot his piece and had to ask for music. The thought of using one's music at the recital never so much as entered the head of one of Lillian Putman's pupils. Every year Daddy and Mother sat through those long recitals. It was a great satisfaction to Daddy to see this bit of evidence that he was giving his children advantages he never had.

On weekday evenings, we went to bed early. Dinner was at noon, so after a lighter meal for supper, we children were soon in bed. The exception to this routine was Wednesday when we went to prayer meeting. This did not alter our sleep schedule, however. David put his head on Mother's lap, and I snuggled close to one or the other of my parents and made a pretense of trying to stay awake. Virginia, since she was so young, could stretch out on a pew in front of, or beside, Mother.

One very warm summer night when there was not enough room close to where we sat, Virginia sleepily stretched out on one of the front rows. Prayer meeting was well under way when Virginia roused herself enough to change to a more comfortable position. In an unconscious move to be cooler, she began to undress. Mother and Daddy watched with dismay as a small yellow dress suddenly appeared over the top of the front seats. Without opening her eyes, Virginia folded the dress neatly on the back of the seat she occupied and settled back to sleep, far more pleasantly situated, no doubt, than anyone else in the congregation.

The prayer meetings most certain to keep me awake were the ones that included church business. These were nearly always exciting. People talked and prayed, but they used a different tone of voice, and they even looked different than they did any other time.

Daddy usually had something to say at business meetings, and it was not always on the winning side. He often spoke in a fine spirit of brotherly love. That is, he did the first time he spoke on a question. There were times when he spoke more than once, and on such occasions his voice would get higher and more tense. And when he sat down, he would rub his hand across his head and clear his throat several times. When this happened, Mother always reached over and patted Daddy on the knee. Since she did it very softly, I think no one could see her except me. It worked the same wonders as a cool breath of air on a hot day. Daddy relaxed a little and sat farther back in his seat.

Daddy's individuality declared itself all through his life. Uncle Doc gives this picture of it: "Marvin . . . did two things his old daddy didn't like: daddy was a strong Methodist but Marvin joined the Baptist Church. Daddy was a 'died in the wool' Democrat yet Marvin voted for Hoover in his first race. Daddy said it was bad enough to be a Baptist. But to be both a Baptist and a Republican was a little more than he could stand."

When the Hundred Thousand Club campaign was organized, I think perhaps Daddy reluctantly agreed to Mother's signing up to help pay the convention debt, but he was unsympathetic. "The whole thing never needed to happen," he said. "And I can't see much hope of any change in how they'll do in the future. We took in over fifty million dollars in the other campaign and now we owe everybody money! We need men with some business sense to head up those boards. Why, if the Sunday School Board was run right, *it* could make money. There's too much waste. Just look at how we do right here in this church—we throw away quarterlies like they didn't cost a cent."

Books and quarterlies were things of great value to Daddy. Our add-a-shelf bookcases at home were full of books he had bought from secondhand bookstores. Daddy was proud of them. He touched them almost reverently. The *Harvard Classics* took up two shelves. The books we bought for study courses at the church were in a neat row. There was a well-worn set of *Compton's Encyclopedia*.

Daddy questioned giving anyone a quarterly free. When we pointed out that some children would have no money to buy them, he said, "All right. Give everybody one apiece. Keep account of who gets them. Then if they want another one, make them pay. That will teach them the value of what they have."

Nor did Daddy take well to the idea of signing a pledge card. Church budgets and pledge cards were very new. To Daddy, budgets were things that made you think you had money when actually you did not. Then you spent money you did not have and ended up in debt. "Like the 75 Million Campaign," he said.

Signing your name to something was like promising your life's blood, in Daddy's way of thinking. And to put the amount of your tithe down on paper was disclosing your income. Daddy would have chosen the rack rather than have a committee looking at the amount of money he made.

The Sunday morning the pastor asked for tithers to sign what they would give every week, Daddy rose from where he sat in our family pew. "In my business, it's impossible to know what I make every week," he said in a strong voice. "I'll give something every Sunday, but I can't sign this card."

My face was hot with embarassment. Your own father getting up in the middle of church! Others followed him, speaking on the tithing question. I cannot remember anything they said.

"Your father ruined our tithing program," a friend told me later. I did not know how to answer her.

Daddy was not a very popular deacon sometimes. Only the Lord knows how much it hurt him to bear the displeasure of his pastor and others of the brethren. But he would not have changed what he did if he had it to do over again. So Daddy never signed a card that revealed his income. He did sign a pledge card finally, when one was printed in a way to which he could honestly put his name. (Eventually, he even let Mother open charge accounts at Russell's Department Store and a few other places. But he never used them. He paid cash.) For Daddy it was hard come, hard go.

In the summer of 1932 came the church split. Rumblings had been heard for some time. Whenever something was discussed in business meeting, argument followed.

Daddy may have argued with his brethren in the church family but to him leaving the church was never the answer. Even if the vote went against you, he felt, you did not quit the field. The church split was something I was almost unaware of until the Sunday it actually happened. Some had felt the church was becoming modernistic. They wanted more old-fashioned gospel preaching like J. Frank Norris delivered in Ft. Worth's First Baptist Church. Some people stayed at home on Sunday during church services so they could hear the great preacher on their radios. They said they had not heard a sermon on the second coming at the church for longer than they liked to remember.

There were hypocrites in the church, too, according to some reports. Even among the deacons there were those who acted one way on Sunday and another way during the week. Now if the church would do some housecleaning and put out from among them these wicked persons, that would be a different situation and perhaps the church would not split after all.

I did not hear these things from my parents. I learned most of them at B.Y.P.U. socials. One of my friends told me the name of a deacon who was doing sinful things the whole town knew about but which the church did nothing about. I did not tell my parents. Since he was their friend, I knew they would be loyal to him no matter what they heard. If I told them what my friend said, they would ask where a teen-ager got information like that and discredit my friend's honesty or intelligence, or both. My parents almost grieved over the idea of a split in the church.

"We need to pray more," Mother would say. I would hear her in her closet praying through many tears.

But one solemn Sunday morning, a lengthy resolution was presented by the leader of the group wanting to form another church. As the names of those asking for their church letters were read, tears began slipping down Mother's cheeks. Daddy rose to his feet to say the letters would be granted in love and forgiveness and understanding.

"And if any of you brethren and your families want to come back and join this church, the doors will always be open," said another deacon.

But in spite of these kind words, a deep wound was opened that day. The departing friends did not form a Southern Baptist Convention church. As the weeks went by, some returned their membership, but most never came back.

Mother and Daddy took us to visit the new church during a revival meeting there. We were welcomed by old friends who urged our parents to consider membership in "a really scriptural Baptist church." Mother and Daddy assured them that the service had been interesting. I do not remember visiting again.

After any Wednesday night business meeting, people lingered longer at church. It was then that business was really transacted, and many times the vote had to be changed at the next meeting. It was an exciting time at church and I enjoyed it. But Mother did not.

On Saturday we began to get ready for Sunday. Mother cleaned the house all morning. In the afternoon she washed our hair. Virginia's hair was put in rag curlers. It came out in long soft curls of pale blond beauty. My hair was cut short and was "cute." When I was queen of the fairies in Miss Crutcher's operetta, I went to the beauty shop for a marcel. The lady took the curling irons from the flame and waved my hair until it stood out all over my head in a most marvelous way. The curl on the ends came out, but the waves stayed in for hours.

When Mother washed her long, red hair, it was something to remember. She rinsed it in rain water which Daddy caught in a bucket from the roof. Mother strained the rain water through a cloth before she used it to make our hair soft.

After Mother dried her hair, she put the towel around her shoulders and went into the back yard to give her hair a sunning. Mother's hair was curly and it gleamed like polished copper in the sun. I thought she was the most beautiful lady in the world. While I watched her brush and fluff her long tresses, I imagined that thousands of people wished they could peek through the vine-covered fence to see her sun her hair. Of course, they would not dare. Only Daddy and we children could see Mother with her hair down.

Our parents rarely went out in the evening. Once in a while there was a social at the church, but unless it was a banquet, the children went too. One hilarious evening the Adult Sunday school department had a suitcase race at their social. We watched in glee our parents and their friends open the suitcases, put on funny looking hats and coats, and race to the end of the basement and back. We laughed until our stomachs ached.

Next door to us lived "Uncle" Lora, "Aunt" Georgia, and their two daughters, who were about our same age. Sometimes Daddy and Mother played Rook with their friends. The five of us children played Rook, too. We played on the floor with the one's, two's, three's and four's. In summer, the four adults played croquet while we played "Wolf over the River" or "New York, New York, what's your trade, lemonade." Mother said they used to play tennis before any of us children were there to see. We found that hard to imagine.

The Rook game would recess temporarily when it was time for Amos and Andy on the radio. Everything stopped for Amos and Andy. When Daddy snapped on the Atwater Kent, squeaks and loud, scratchy noises came from the big horn-like speaker. But Daddy kept tuning, and we got Amos and Andy. We were quieter then in our play. The grownups laughed at Amos and Andy and talked afterward about the marvel of radio.

One evening Daddy and Mother went to the corner to visit the Baileys, who had sickness in their home. For lack of something better to do, I turned on the radio. After experimental tuning, there came from the speaker rhythmic, stirring music such as I had never heard before. I clapped my hands to it and waved my arms in a pretence of directing the orchestra. When I could keep in one spot no longer, I called to David and Virginia. "Let's march around!" I cried. I led, and they followed me. The music put wings on our feet. We marched up and down the room. We circled faster and faster while the music soared around our heads.

In the midst of this reveling, Mother and Daddy came home. We fell on them and told them what fun we had with the beautiful music. "And I know what it is so we can get it again," I said. "It's called dance orchestra music. Oh, don't you just love it!"

"How can I hear you with the music so loud?" Mother asked. But when she touched the radio, she turned it off, not down. I looked at Daddy. He said nothing, but I could tell he did not like the music.

"Time for bed," said Mother. "Tomorrow is Sunday."

3

Now I'm Found

It is not really long after February until April comes. It just seems long. March is cold and the wind blows so. And there are never any out-of-season warm days to build up your hope.

But all of a sudden it is April. The skies turn blue, the grass begins to green, and the wind blows just as hard, but it comes from the south and east. Long underwear, which felt pretty good during March, begins to stick to you, and even Mother cannot hold out in April.

"All right, Connie Betty," she says, "I'll cut off some of your old union suits in case the days become very warm."

That is all it takes. Snip, snip, snip, and off come the sleeves right at the shoulder seams. Two more whacks of the scissors and one leg is off. Two more snips and I am free as a bird.

Then Mother puts a cherry on top of the whipped cream. "I have bought you some socks," she says, pulling some elastic out of her Chinese sewing basket. (The blue silk tassels are gone, but the beads are still there.) "Here, let me measure your knees and I'll make your garters."

Around my knee she puts the elastic and cuts it to fit. Then she measures another piece with the cut one. Her needle flies as she sews each piece together. When I slip them on over my new socks, they fit firmly under the folds just below my knees. Even the old lace up shoes do not matter now. The union suits are mortally wounded for a long spring and summer. It is April!

The horned toads come out. The baby ones are no bigger than

Daddy's thumb nail, and only small nimble fingers can catch their tiny tails. Their underside is smooth and soft. It goes up and down, up and down with every breath and heart beat; when they are on the ground again, they scurry away. It makes you smile to see them. You look up, and the blue, blue, blue Oklahoma sky smiles back at you. So do the little white, white, white clouds. They look like fleecy lambs—not the kind of lambs you see from car windows as you go down a highway, but the kind you see on calendars—white as pearls. Nothing—do you hear?—absolutely nothing is prettier than a blue Oklahoma sky filled with little white clouds on a warm day in April.

There may be one thing more beautiful. It is a night in summer when all the stars come out. You can see more of them from our back yard in Altus than any place else on this earth. Maybe on Mars there will be a better view, but not here. When the sun goes down, Daddy gets out the hose and sprinkles the vines that cling to the fence, and the grass, not enough to get it soggy wet, but just enough to get the dust off good and make it feel cool and soft under your feet.

The telephone rings and Daddy goes into the house to talk about the price of wheat. The whole back yard is yours. Night is dark light, and the stars are out in full force. The moon is not shiny. It is softly silver with shimmering music coming down. The music goes into your heart and catches your feet. It sets them dancing all over the yard. You can dance on your toes to music like this. And just look how beautiful your hands are! You know for sure there are not any fairies, but they come anyway. They dance all around you, and everywhere they go there is color—the kind you can see through. Oh, when the moonlight comes through the colors it is a lovely thing!

"Daughter," says Daddy, coming out to see about watering the vines, "what are you doing out here? I think Mother wants you in the house."

School kept in April, of course. But at recess there were jumping ropes, even double jumping ropes for flying feet and bare knees. Every girl at Washington Ward School had a set of jacks.

The lucky ones had golf balls to go with their jacks, and they received permission to play on the cement sidewalk which separated the boys' side of the playground from the girls' side. Sometimes the boys would manage to slip over to the sidewalk to watch a game, and *then* the birds were really put in the nest without a miss or you were simply disgraced.

There was dust, too, in April. It was not so bad while I was in Washington Ward School. It was bad during the thirties, when I was in high school. Then the dust really came. It came rolling in across the plains like a huge tidal wave. If you wanted to, you could watch it coming, but when it got close enough for you to hear the roaring wind, you ran inside and shut the door.

The worst dust was the silent kind. Early in the morning a dark, dismal sky would sift the dust down without a sound and without a wisp of wind. There was not room enough to breathe between your head and the sky.

We were the lucky ones, for we lived in town and it was not our land blowing away. But it was our neighbor's land, and what hurt them hurt us a little too. Our house was sturdy and made of plaster. The windows and doors were tight and strong, but when Mother cleaned house it did no good. The grey, silent dust crept in where there was no place to get in, and soon only a small hump told where the carpet ended and the hardwood floor began. The dust was over everything, grey and fine and gritty.

Mother cried sometimes because she was made for clean houses, and she did not mind working hard to make them clean. But nothing kept them clean when the dust came.

One day Daddy came to where she stood looking out a window. "Mother," he said, "the geese change their home and God takes care of them. He'll take care of us, too. You just tell me what you want to do, and we'll do it. There are plenty of places on God's earth for us to live."

Mother shook her head and wiped her tears on the back of her hand. She went to the closet and took out the vacuum. That was in the thirties. I do not remember much dust while I was in grade school.

I remember cyclones. They came every year. Well, they did not really quite get to our house, but they came close enough to scare the teeth and toenails off you.

Daddy was the chief storm cloud watcher for the neighborhood. We did not have a cyclone cellar but we were welcome to use the Bailey's any time.

Mother Bailey had grandchildren. And since she knew all about caring for sick babies, everyone called her Mother Bailey. Daddy said she helped take care of me during my second summer when I almost died with summer complaint.

Many a day and night found us in the Bailey's big storm cellar. It was made of cement and had a little chimney for air to get in and out. Most storm cellars were dug out of the earth, with the earth on top held up by boards. Each cellar had a wooden door almost flat on the ground which was kept open during the day except during storms. Steps went straight down into the cellar where a kerosene lamp was the only light in the dark.

It was scary to go down into the cellar at night. But it was scarier not to go, especially at night. If it was a warmer night than usual and there was not a breath of air stirring and if clouds hung low and heavy, Daddy quietly pushed open the back screen door to take a look at the sky. I always heard him. Without waking Virginia, I crept to the window and watched Daddy, his long white night shirt a spot of light in the dark yard, looking at the sky. I always began hoping right then we would go to the storm cellar. If the cloud looked bad enough, Daddy hurried into the house.

"We'd better go to the cellar, Mother," he said. "Get the children."

Then, with our hearts thumping fast, we were bundled into coats and shoes. "No socks, children. Just get on your shoes," Mother pleaded. "Hurry!"

Sometimes the fire whistle blew to wake the town to danger. When we got to the cellar, there were likely to be others already there. Daddy called to neighbors on the way. When all the ladies and children were in and the lamps were lit, the men stood just outside the door. If the cloud went over or around, or just disappeared, the men laughed and called to the ladies, and everyone would tease about the false alarm and go home to bed. If the cloud came in, the men would suddenly rush into the cellar. Daddy was the last one in. He and Mr. Bailey tugged on the rope and pulled the door down securely as the wind tore overhead with a great roar. No one tried to talk until the rain began to fall. When the rain tapered off to a gentle drizzle, Daddy and Mr. Bailey opened the door and looked at the sky.

"That one was close enough to scare the teeth and toenails off a person," said Daddy as we walked home.

The storms did come close. Nine miles to the north, people were killed and brick buildings torn to bits. Another day, a cyclone came through farm country a few miles to the east. The next Sunday afternoon we joined the many who came out of curiosity to see a new steel bridge which was twisted out of shape. The bridge was blocked off, and uniformed state troopers from Oklahoma City directed traffic. We followed the stream of cars down a dusty road past what was left of a farm house. Not much was left. The foundation of the house covered with shreds of wood was still there, but the rest was scattered along the path of the cyclone. "A man and woman were killed there," said Daddy.

"I want to go home," said David.

"We're going home," said Mother. "But you children mustn't get scared about cyclones. The Indians say Altus will never blow away because it's too high. That's why they called it Altus—it means high."

What a comfort those Indians were to me, they will never know. I did not wonder where Mother discovered their prediction about Altus. I supposed it was at Grandmother's house. Grandmother Connie Holland lived at Shawnee. Indians lived there—fat, silent, dark people with braided hair and new cars. Grandfather David Holland—a handsome, white-haired, giant of a man—said the Indians struck oil and were the richest people in

Oklahoma. Grandfather David ran for land when Oklahoma was opened to white people, but his land did not have oil.

"It had lots of weeds though," laughed Grandfather. "The Indians never wanted my land. You know what they did want from me? They wanted your mother because she had red hair. Tried to trade me right out of her—had to watch night and day to keep them from stealing her."

"That was Texas Indians, Grandpa," said Grandmother Connie. "Now you quit scarin' the children."

We were not scared, but we always looked at Mother with admiring eyes after Grandfather told the familiar story. He and Grandmother came from Arkansas to Texas in a covered wagon. It was while they were crossing Texas that the Indians appeared and asked to trade for their first born, two-year-old Alva Lee with hair the color of polished copper.

That was a long, long time ago and, besides, those were Texas Indians. And Mother, her shining hair pulled softly to a big round loop at the back of her neck, was safe with us. Since she was an authority on Indians, if she said the Indians cleared Altus from having cyclones, why that was that.

The storms came close, and the whole town was jittery. "Easter is late this year," said Daddy, "so there'll be more storms."

Easter was only a few days away. I had a new pair of white slippers, and Mother was sewing me a dress of lavender silk with a white lace bertha collar. The bridal wreath was blooming along the way to school.

"Remember Junior choir practice this afternoon," said Mother.

Altus First Church was blessed with really fine "singers," as we called our ministers of music. Everyone was sorry when Brother Huber moved away. A Texas church called him for their singer, but he and Mrs. Huber visited occasionally when they came back to sing for weddings.

The singer I remember best was Brother George. "We're certainly fortunate to have people like the Reynolds," said Mother. We agreed. We liked William and Richard, the Reynolds' sons.

Mrs. Reynolds could play both the piano and the organ. How we sang when Brother George led and Mrs. Reynolds played! Brother George even got the church to buy new hymnbooks. He taught us new songs, and when we sang the old ones out of the new books, they even sang better.

At Junior choir, we soon discovered that Brother George did not put up with any foolishness. We sat up straight, we listened, we sang.

"Now on this next verse," said Brother George, "I want you to whistle."

Whistle! At Junior choir? I was not sure I wanted to. I decided to be uncertain that I could.

"Why didn't you whistle?" Brother George looked at me. So did everyone else.

"I don't know how to whistle," I pouted.

"Wheist," said Brother George, "I wouldn't give a nickle for a girl who couldn't whistle." He started the next song and ignored me.

I was indignant. Not worth a nickel indeed! I would never come back to Junior choir—never! I would tell my mother! I would tell my mother nothing, as I very well knew. Mother would ask why I did not whistle, and say, "Next time you mind him, young lady." Next time Brother George asked us to whistle, I found I could do a fair job of it.

Mrs. Reynolds helped me learn to play hymns. She told me to play them reverently, and showed me how. One Sunday Brother George asked me to play the piano for the church service. Mrs. Reynolds was at the organ. I missed cues, I played wrong notes, but he asked me to play again.

I still wonder at Brother George's patience—not patience that endured things, but patience that accomplished things. With Brother George there, things happened. We became a singing congregation. The choir was filled with willing voices. Young men began coming down the aisle to dedicate their lives to full-time Christian service in music. Any boy in the church felt it was an honor to be elected chorister.

Brother George had us elect a high school boy for chorister at B.Y.P.U. general assembly. Then how we sang! People who were gathering in the main auditorium for the Sunday night service said they never heard such singing. When general assembly was over, we streamed into the auditorium still humming the chorus we had been taught that night.

When the depression came, Brother George kept on singing. "Thou whose riches are in glory, stand by me," Brother George sang. It made tears come into our eyes. We knew Brother George understood. It helped for him to sing "Stand by Me."

On Easter Sunday we always sang "Low in the Grave He Lay." We would sing it this Easter Sunday, softly on the verses, and then everyone would burst out on "Up from the grave He arose, with a mighty triumph o'er His foes." It sent a shiver of delight up my back just to think of it.

Easter was the best time of the year. It was the day Christ arose. It was the day people smiled at each other and the organ played "Christ the Lord is risen today, Alleluia!" It was a time to think about the angel coming down, rolling the stone away, and sitting on it.

"Every Sunday is Easter Sunday for Baptists," our parents taught us, "because every Sunday is when we remember Christ is alive and with us always." We knew that, but somehow we knew too that on Easter Sunday we rejoiced a little more than usual about it.

No Easter bunny visited our house. I have a faint memory of an Easter egg hunt somewhere on Sunday afternoon, but it was not a traditional part of our celebration. I do not think our parents disapproved of such things. It seems more likely there was not time to add another event to those full Sunday mornings. So we were blessed with a sacred holiday to be celebrated in the simplicity of a single thought: It was the day Christ arose from the dead.

There was great excitement getting ready for Sunday school on Easter. New shoes are hard to button, and the sash of a new dress ties differently from the old one. Daddy did not have new clothes, but he pinned a flower on his lapel. On Mother's Day, he had a tear in his eye as he pinned on a white rose in memory of his dear little mother, our Grandmother Betty. But on Easter, the flower could be any color. We made it to church just as the bell rang.

Everybody was at Sunday school. Everybody wore something new. Or if they did not wear something new, they wore an air of not believing in wearing anything new on Easter, which worked just as well. It was the day everyone looked cleaner and smelled sweeter than any other Sunday.

For the preaching service we sat in our family pew and admired all the flowers at the front of the church. We were more wiggly than usual, and Virginia and I kept telling David to move over so we could have more room to fluff our skirts around us.

"Let us turn to page 55," announced the singer, "and sing 'Christ Arose.'"

We sang it while people, more people than usual, kept coming in for church. Everyone picked up a hymnbook and swelled the music with glad voices.

"Now let us sing a song to help us understand what Easter really means: number 37, 'Amazing Grace.'"

Daddy took off his glasses and put them in his pocket. It was not so easy for him to keep pace when we sang "up from the grave He arose," but "Amazing Grace" he knew by heart. Off key, but by heart.

> Amazing grace! how sweet the sound,
>   That saved a wretch like me!
> I once was lost, but now am found,
>   Was blind, but now I see.

Straight to my heart went those words "I once was lost but now am found." I love Jesus, I told myself, so I must not be lost. But am I found?

Brother Burton preached. I do not remember what he preached about that day. Mother said it did not matter what

Brother Burton said. "If he just stood there and said 'twinkle, twinkle little star,' you'd feel the Holy Spirit and tears would come to your eyes." Brother Burton was a man of God. You felt God when he preached. After he finished, the invitation began. It was "Just as I Am."

> Just as I am, without one plea,
> But that Thy blood was shed for me,
> And that Thou bidd'st me come to Thee,
> O Lamb of God, I come, I come!

No one came down the aisle on the first verse. *Why don't I go?* The second verse was beginning. Brother Burton stood close to the aisle, waiting. *I don't need to go. I am too young. I can trust Jesus without going to the front.*

> Just as I am, and waiting not

But people who love Jesus do go down to the front. That's the way they show they have trusted him to save them from their sins. If I loved him, I would go.

If I loved him! But I did, I did! Tears began pouring down my cheeks. I started edging my way past my parents to the aisle.

"Connie, what are you doing?" asked Mother.

"I am going to trust Jesus," I sobbed.

Daddy heard me. He lifted me up and kissed my cheek and helped me into the aisle.

> O Lamb of God, I come, I come.

Brother Burton met me at the front. The singer started the congregation on another verse of the invitation.

Brother Burton asked me if I was trusting Jesus. He asked if I understood why I needed to trust Jesus. Did I know I was lost without him? Did I know he would save me forever? Brother Burton sat on the edge of the platform in front of the pulpit to talk to me. I was a Primary, and I was undersized for even a

Primary. Brother Burton put his arm around me. "Let's pray and tell the Lord about it," he said. While the congregation sang, Brother Burton talked to God about me and thanked God that I had come to trust Jesus.

"This is Brother and Sister Moore's little girl, Connie Betty," Brother Burton told the congregation after they finished the hymn and were seated. "She is very young, but she has come to say she is trusting Jesus as her personal Saviour. Is that the way it is, Connie Betty?"

I nodded my head. He asked other questions, helping me to say what I felt in my heart. "And do you want to follow Christ in baptism and become a member of this church?"

My heart pounded with anticipation. "Oh yes, I do," I answered quickly.

Brother Burton addressed the congregation. "Now, of course, Connie Betty will discuss this with her parents and with me to be sure she thoroughly understands the step she is taking. You have heard her reasons for presenting herself to us. Do I hear a motion that after her baptism she be accepted into church membership?"

A deacon so moved. Someone seconded the motion.

"All who are in favor, say aye," said Brother Burton.

"Aye," said the church.

"All who are opposed, say nay."

There was no sound.

"Let us stand for the benediction," said Brother Burton. "I'm sure you'll want to come give Connie Betty the right hand of Christian fellowship, so I will ask her to stand here at the front after we have our word of prayer."

Brother Burton prayed and church was over. In an instant I felt Mother's arms around me and her wet check next to mine. Daddy stood beside her clearing his throat and telling Mr. Russell that, yes, he was proud. Mrs. Russell kissed me and so did Mother Bailey. Aunt Georgia kissed Mother and they both cried and told each other the Lord answers prayer.

It seemed to me that everyone in the church came to give me

the right hand of Christian fellowship. Dr. Abernathy said, "God
bless you," when he shook my hand. Judge Austin was solemn
as he passed. Miss Flora said it would not be long now till she
had me in her Junior department. Mrs. Pendleton, right behind
her in line, said she hoped I was in her Sunday school class next
year and that she would be praying for me as I began my Christian life. Mrs. Briscoe started to say something, but she patted
my shoulder instead. Mr. Briscoe said, "We're sure glad, Connie
Betty."

Everyone made me feel glad as they shook my hand. I had a
warm, hushed feeling, and I could not say a word for the wonder
of it all.

Aunt Georgia and Uncle Lora and the girls had Sunday dinner with us after church. At the table I was included in the
adult conversation. Uncle Lora told about the day he was saved
and joined the church.

"It was Dr. Truett in Dallas that got me to thinking about it,"
said Daddy. "When I left home in Tennessee to go west, I never
dreamed how lonesome I'd be in Texas. I'd go to church to hear
Dr. Truett pray. He always prayed for the boys away from home.
There were a lot of boys in Dallas who were away from home,
but I felt like Dr. Truett was praying especially for me.

"My little Methodist mother had held me in her arms and had
me sprinkled when I was a baby. She died when I was a little
boy and I knew she couldn't pray for me anymore. I just couldn't
get away from Dr. Truett's prayers though, and one night when
I was selling on the road, I stopped at the First Baptist Church
in Waco and made my profession of faith in Jesus Christ. I told
the preacher I wanted to be baptized right then, that very night.
He said, 'Why, young man, the water is as cold as ice, and besides you don't have any clothes to be baptized in.'

"I said, 'Preacher, I've got the ones I have on.' So he baptized
me that very night. I walked back to my boarding house in wet
clothes, but I was never so happy in my life."

Mother had been saved when she was a little girl. She told
about how she began teaching a class of Junior girls when she

was fourteen and had been teaching in Sunday school ever since.

"The day I was saved I saw angels standing all around," said Aunt Georgia. "I know you won't believe it, but I did. I never did before or since, but I saw angels that day."

"Maybe you were like the apostle Paul," said Mother. "He saw a great light and heard the Lord speak when he was saved. Not everyone has the same experience."

In the days that followed, Mother tried to help me in my new experience. She urged me to read my Bible every day and to pray. But to me, the Bible was something to carry to church every Sunday and something with memory verses in it. I knew it contained sixty-six books. I could name them, but I could not spell them, of course. I could sing the names of the apostles and I could quote the Lord's Prayer and the twenty-third Psalm. My favorite memory verse was "What time I am afraid, I will trust in thee." I said it to myself in the dark one night after dreaming that the school building was on fire.

Once I had not dreamed, but I woke in the dark. (Did a board creak?) In front of my wide-opened, searching eyes, the folds of the blankets looked like a man's cap. In a split second, my imagination put the cap on a robber's head, and there he was with a gun, right beside my head! I screamed, and Mother and Daddy bounded out of their bed to come running to my aid.

With the flick of a light switch, all such robbers vanish, you know, and so did mine. Daddy trudged back to bed and Mother tucked me in again. "Now you just think of daffodils in a meadow with pretty butterflies around them, and then you won't have bad dreams," she comforted.

I started to explain that it was not a dream, but the middle of the night is not a good time to explain. "And remember," said Mother as she gave a last pat, " 'What time I am afraid, I will trust in thee.' "

I think I did not realize that I prayed often, spontaneously talking to God, in my heart. I had one vibrant experience with the kind of prayer you think about before you pray. It happened on a sunny afternoon when I was five years old.

That afternoon Mother went to a neighbor's house to sew. The neighbor was the favorite lady of the whole block. She made cookies. She made cookies that you ate between meals. Her cookies, moreover, were available at any time one happened past her back door. There was a well-beaten path to her back door. David in first trying to say "Mrs. Gilbert" came out with something that sounded like "Budder," and Budder she had been ever since.

Mother interrupted her sewing with Budder that afternoon and called me to her. "I have forgotten my scissors, Connie. Please go over and bring them to me. They are either in my sewing basket or in a drawer in the dining room. Remember to *walk* back over here and carry the scissors with the points down."

Mother told us over and over how to carry scissors. I ran to our house and looked around where the scissors usually were put. I opened drawer after drawer. The scissors were not to be found. Mother probably had them with her all the time and had discovered them by now. I was having a delightful time at Budder's playing with Erma Ruth's paper dolls, and I was anxious to get back.

Erma Ruth was being extra nice to me because Budder found out about the last time we played paper dolls. I was a nuisance to Erma Ruth and her older friend Kathleen, so she had cut the heads off several paper dolls and told me to go play with *them*. I cried and cried, and for some reason Daddy took up for me. He was very angry.

"I'll build a fence between these houses," Daddy said in such a loud voice the whole neighborhood heard it. I do not know exactly what happened after that except Daddy never built a fence. And later when Erma Ruth had pneumonia, he sat up all night with her.

Anyhow, things were fine today. I flew back to tell Mother I could not find the scissors.

Mother sighed. "If it had been a snake it would have bitten you. I'm sure you put your hand right on them if you looked where I told you. I suppose I'll have to get them myself."

Budder put a restraining hand on Mother's knee. She looked

at me and said softly, "Did you ask the Lord to help you find them? Why don't you try again and pray the Lord's help?"

I have no reason to believe I was not a conscious sinner from that moment on. I rebelled at the idea of praying. How humiliating to be asked to pray about scissors!

"I don't want to," I said flippantly, and started back to my paper dolls.

If I had been respectful in refusing, I think Mother would have told me to run along play while she got the scissors herself. But Mother did not cotton to young ladies being uppity to adults. Her eyes snapped. "Connie Betty, go to the house again. This time you take time to look good. Then you carefully bring me the scissors."

There was no back talk when Mother looked like that. I ran to our house and, still panting, began to look for the scissors. I would find them all right, but nobody could make me pray about it—nobody—never, never, never!

But I could not find them. I looked frantically. I looked everywhere. I looked everywhere again. I must find them. If I went back without them, I would be asked, "Did you pray?" I either had to find them or pray.

I could not find them. I stood alone in the house, quiet and still, and knew I had to pray. I went over behind the door and asked, "Dear God, please help me find the scissors."

I pulled open the top drawer of the buffet, reached inside, and had the scissors in my hand.

A wonder seized my heart. God had helped me! Now I wanted to pray; I even wanted to kneel. "Oh thank you, dear God," I whispered. I felt, from that afternoon, that God could answer prayer the way I wanted him to answer it. I soon found that he did not always do so. Prayer was a strange thing.

One day in the week following Easter, Mother came to my room. "Darling," she said, "would you like to read the Bible with me today?"

"Oh, all right," I said unenthusiastically.

Mother read some verses and got on her knees. I knelt beside her. She prayed. She prayed for me and asked the Lord to help me in my new life in him.

"Would you like to pray now, too?" she asked.

I knew I should say yes. But I did not want to pray. I knew I should pray just a few words to be respectful to Mother, but I rebelled. "No," I said. "I don't want to."

"That's all right," said Mother. We both got up and Mother left me and went to her housework.

I was miserable. Why had I said I would not pray? Why did I not want to pray? Maybe I was not saved at all. Anyone who loved and trusted Jesus should want to pray. I must still be lost —lost and going to hell when I died.

With a sob I fell down beside my bed. "All right, God!" I cried. "All right! So I'm going to hell! But you just remember this: When I'm down in hell I'm still going to be trusting Jesus—I'll keep right on loving him all the time I'm there!"

I did not see any angels and there was no light from heaven. No voice came to my ear; but at that moment I knew more surely than I knew I was breathing that God was not going to send me to hell—no, not ever. I could not see him, but he was with me, and he understood things I could not even ask. I once was lost, but now I knew certainty that filled my whole being with peace. **I was found.**

4

Summertime

Vacations and holidays were family affairs at our house. In the early fall we went to the country to pick up pecans and to admire the red leaves of the sumac bushes. Or we drove a few miles to the east of Altus and went mountain climbing. Daddy knew the way to the top of the highest of the granite mountains. Mother and Virginia went to the first resting place and stayed until Daddy and David and I climbed to the top and back.

What beauty we saw from the top! Miles of plains swept out below us. How pretty was the little river winding through the fields! The fields themselves looked like one of Mother's quilts. Squares of different colored material—green winter wheat, brown fresh-turned soil, rows of cotton stubs, and waving alfalfa—lay over the horizon. The sun, about to go down, glazed the little river like a shiny mirror. I liked to sit at the top of the mountain and just look. It made me feel good inside.

The week before Christmas, we came to the mountains to find a cedar tree. Daddy brought his Scout hatchet and chopped away in the cold wind. What a gay parade we made coming down with our Christmas tree!

One Christmas, Daddy told us a law had been passed to protect the trees on the mountains. "It's a good law," he sighed. "We'll buy a tree this year." The trees we bought each year after that were more symmetrical and looked like Christmas trees should look. But, oh, the smell of a fresh cedar tree in the house, for Christmas was something to remember!

School was out the last of May, and anytime afterwards we were apt to make trips. If Daddy needed to go to Oklahoma City on business, we went along. We left before daylight and ate breakfast on the way. Beside some tree or creek, Daddy pulled the car over to a stop. Mother unpacked things she brought—a skillet, bacon, eggs, a coffee pot, and coffee.

Daddy and David gathered sticks for a fire. Daddy could start a fire without matches, but he usually remembered the matches and used them. Daddy made a fine camp fire. It blazed high for a few moments and simmered down just right for Mother to put the skillet over it. Daddy fixed the coffee pot on a forked stick over the fire. The fire smoked up the pot, but it was an old, enameled one, used only for this. The coffee was soon boiling away, bacon was sending out heavenly aroma, and I tell you for sure, you never in all your life tasted scrambled eggs as good as the ones Mother fixed in bacon grease over a campfire! It would have been a crime to have had only one apiece. Mother kept breaking egg after egg and whipping the gooey mass into a frothy, golden delight. Then she spooned them into the pie-tin plates we used for picnics. We bowed our heads while Daddy thanked the Lord for the good food and the great outdoors which he had created for us to enjoy.

We ate three times as much as we ate at home. This pleased Mother, whose face was almost as red as her hair from holding the skillet over the fire. She pushed back a damp curl from her forehead and drank a long draught of coffee. "It's worth it," she said.

Daddy enjoyed these times to the full. He called strange sounds into the air, and soon a bird would be answering from a tree in the distance. When we finished eating, he carefully covered the camp fire with earth, and we were on our way again.

While Daddy transacted business in the city, we stayed in the car and waited. Or Daddy left us uptown to shop. After such shopping trips, Daddy vowed he would never bring the family to the city again. We spent too much money, and he was sure if we had been home, we would not have bought a thing.

"Maybe not today, but sooner or later," Mother told Daddy.

"We can't afford it," Daddy answered. He always said that.

"Now, Marvin," said Mother, "you know the children have to have things."

Daddy knew and he did not really mind. It made him feel better if he said in a loud voice, "We can't afford it!"

There was one time he meant it. It was the first and last time I bought some "popular" sheet music. I begged Mother to let me get some Bing Crosby songs. Finally, Mother said, "Well, all right, just this once."

The music had bright yellow front pages with pictures of Bing Crosby and Joan Bennett. Daddy could not help noticing the bright-yellow music. He saw the pictures of movie stars on the front and roared, "Did your piano teacher tell you to get that kind of music to practice on?"

"N-no, sir," I said, "but . . ."

"We don't spend money on picture-show music. That isn't the kind I want you to play. The movies are getting rich off poor people who don't have sense enough to leave that kind of stuff alone!"

I burst into tears and Mother sat with her back straight and her eyes snapping. But everyone in the family knew how Daddy felt about picture shows and their kind of music. I thought I could get by with this because Daddy was lenient to the point of extravagance when it came to my music. Now I knew there was music and music. Anyway, I became quite adept at playing popular music by ear.

When all the business and the shopping were finished in Oklahoma City, we went to see Grandmother in Shawnee or to Uncle Oscar and Aunt Selma's house in Jones. Uncle Oscar said Jones was the biggest little city in the world. He had a lumberyard there. Aunt Selma was Mother's youngest sister, and her hair was almost as red as Mother's. She made fudge soft as velvet. It was filled with rich pecans, and she always cut it in big squares.

Once I spent a whole blissful week alone with Aunt Selma and

Uncle Oscar. I played miniature golf every day on a course across from the lumberyard. We went into the city and ate hamburgers at a restaurant close to the capitol. I did not think the capitol was very pretty with oil derricks in front of it and Alfalfa Bill's crops around it.

"It's the depression," said Uncle Oscar.

There was no miniature golf at Grandmother's house in Shawnee, but she had an upstairs front porch. A door on the second floor opened out on the porch. The little balustrade around it looked like icing on a bakery cookie. "It is old," said Mother. "If you fell against it, it might break right off." She locked the door and did I know not what with the key.

Between Grandmother's dining room and living room was a heavy, dark-red, fish-net curtain. It arched high in the middle, and all along the arch dangled long, fat tassels. It was beautiful to behold, and we ran back and forth under it touching the tassels with our hands.

"Now, you leave the children alone," Grandmother told Mother. "Let them have a good time."

We had a good time. At Grandmother's house we looked for pins. If we found one, we called to Grandmother. She came to where we stood and determined whether or not the pin was pointing toward us. This was important. "If a pin points toward you, you'll have good luck," said Grandmother Connie.

Out in the back, Grandmother kept chickens. Every morning we listened to where the rooster stood when he crowed. "There'll be company today if the rooster crows at the door," Grandmother said. She could even tell what kind of company was coming. If she dropped a fork, a man was coming; if she dropped a knife, it was a woman coming for sure. And if a spoon hit the floor, there would be a child. These signs always came to pass. There was always company when Grandmother dropped things. "I've never seen it to fail yet," said Grandmother Connie.

Down the street a few blocks from her house was the Bison Theater. We went to more picture shows on short visits to Grandmother's than we ever did at home.

"Now, Marvin," said Grandmother real sassy-like. Nobody talked to Daddy like Grandmother. "You let those children go to the picture show. It's not going to hurt them. You were young once yourself."

Daddy rubbed his hand over his head. "All right," he said, "I guess that's so." And off we went with Uncle Bryan or Uncle Carl or some other of our older kin.

Our stays with Grandmother and Grandfather Holland were the short but sweet kind. Daddy was always in a hurry to get home. But while we were there, he talked often and respectfully to his mother- and father-in-law.

Long ago, when Daddy came to take Mother away to be married, Grandfather Holland told him, "You be sure you get a Baptist preacher and no other kind to marry you."

Daddy did just that. He and Mother went to Chickasaw and were married by the pastor of the First Baptist Church there. They waited until the morning service was over and approached the pastor to ask him to perform the ceremony. Daddy was a nervous groom, and he hoped no one would know what was going on. But a little boy heard him talking to the preacher. The boy ran out and yelled to the departing congregation, "There's going to be a wedding—a wedding! Come back!"

The next day, early in the morning, Daddy left his bride in a small hotel while he went about his day's work. "I'll have your breakfast sent up to the room," he told the very new Mrs. J. M. Moore.

Downstairs in the dining room, he ordered Mother's breakfast. "Now send that up to Miss Alva Holland," he told the boy.

At noon he returned to a very hungry and unhappy bride. Daddy's consternation knew no bounds when he learned Mother received no breakfast. He stormed downstairs to demand explanations for the outrage.

"But sir," he was told, "there is no Miss Alva Holland registered here." Poor Daddy never lived that down.

Grandmother Holland belonged to the Christian church. She was a Baptist, first. Shortly after she was baptized, her pastor was found guilty of stealing forty bushels of corn. The deacons decided everyone who was baptized by the bad preacher must be rebaptized to stay in the church. Grandmother refused. "He hadn't stole anything when he baptized me," she said. "There was nothing wrong with my baptism."

The deacons insisted, so grandmother joined the Christian church. We did not blame her a bit. We admired her spunk. And we loved to visit her.

We had the most fun on family trips in Oklahoma when we went to Camp Boulder in the forest reservation of the Wichita Mountains. Camp Boulder is the camp site just beyond Lost Lake as you come in the southwest gate of the reservation. Going in, we passed buffalo herds behind their protective fences.

"You children take a good look," said Daddy, "because you won't be seeing wild buffalo many more years."

We looked in awe at the shaggy-headed creatures, but we never wanted to look very long. "Let's go on," we cried. "Let's get to the swimming place!" That was always the best part—to swim and swim and swim!

Camp Boulder was near the entrance of a canyon. A clear, clean stream ran through the bottom of the canyon, and in this stream we did our swimming. As more and more people discovered Camp Boulder, we went farther back into the canyon to find our swimming pool. This pleased Daddy, who loved to hike and explore. Clad in his black swim suit, which buttoned at the shoulders and boasted a flapping skirt above its short pants, he led us down the canyon, pointing out its beautiful colors in the sheer cliffs on either side. We walked along the granite boulders or waded through the stream.

Mother bought canvas, rubber-soled shoes to protect our feet. She told us over and over to keep a towel around our shoulders so we would not get sunburned. But we always got sunburned. It was hot and a towel around our shoulders made it hotter. So we forgot every time. For days after a hike down the canyon, we were miserable with sunburn. Our skin turned a raw pink-red, changed into blisters, and in a few days we peeled off.

Far down the canyon, Daddy pointed out the eagle's nest. It perched on the bank of the highest part of the canyon. "Now, that is a sight worth seeing," said Daddy.

"Let's swim, Daddy," we pleaded. "This is a good place." The stream beneath the canyon was a deep, clear blue-green.

"Well, now, we'll just see," said Daddy. He took off his shoes and began to wade into the stream. Suddenly, he disappeared under the water. He came up sputtering and treading water. "There's a jumping off place here," said Daddy. "No telling how deep it is! Let me see if I can find out."

With a lunge of his arms, he went under the water. We waited breathlessly until his head shot up through the water again. "Can't even touch bottom," he shouted. "This is a Jim Dandy!"

"Now, Marvin, be careful," Mother cautioned.

"Can we come in?" we called eagerly. "Let us—let us!"

"Now, you wait just a minute," Daddy warned. He swam around until his feet touched the sandy bottom of the stream. He waded and swam back and forth testing the depth of the water and feeling for rocks.

"You can dive into the deep water from that rock over there," Daddy pointed to a high boulder with a smooth side plunging straight into the stream. "Be careful over here because you can't stop until you cross over to the sandy side." Daddy was treading water while he talked to us. "You can dive in now, and I'll be here to catch you if you need me."

With whoops of joy we dived or held our noses and jumped into the water. We did not need Daddy to catch us, but we jumped harder and farther because we knew he was there.

Mother did not dive in. She said diving turned her liver over. She pushed herself smoothly into the water and swam across the pool. Daddy surface-dived and touched her foot.

Mother screamed. "There are fish in here, Marvin! Something bit me! Marvin!"

Daddy was up now behind her in the water. He began to laugh and we joined in. Mother laughed too, but she said indignantly, "It isn't funny."

We took turns riding on Daddy's back while he swam across the deep hole where he could not touch bottom. "I don't see any sense in doing that," said Mother. "There is plenty of water over here where it's safer."

"Now, Mother, I'm going to take care of them," said Daddy, but we knew very well he would not let us in the deep pool if Mother was not there to worry about us.

Those days under the hot, clear Oklahoma sky, we were a family. We could not have explained it to anyone, but we felt the bond of blood and love among us which was stronger than an army with banners.

The most exciting trips we took together were the ones we made to visit Daddy's relatives in Tennessee. These trips took three days going, three days to visit, and three days returning.

"Three days," said Daddy, "is long enough to visit anybody."

The three days we visited in Tennessee were very important ones. Mother washed, starched, and ironed every ruffle and collar. On one trip, I remember, Mother got three new dresses in Nashville before we arrived at our relatives' homes. One was beaded all over with black jets that turned different colors in the light. Another one had fringe all around. Daddy got new shoes, which were very hard for him to find because they had to be quite wide, especially for his left foot. After Mother insisted with sparks in her eyes, Daddy bought a new, white summer suit, too.

When we were very young and paved highways in Oklahoma and Arkansas were rare, we took our cots and spent the nights en route beside a stream or in some meadow under the stars. But later, when fences bore signs saying "KEEP OUT," we stayed in tourist courts.

If we traveled on Sunday, we stopped for Sunday school and church in whatever town we found ourselves at the time. That is, every time except one Sunday. On this Sunday we were running behind schedule. We got off a day later than Daddy first planned, and he was anxious to make up time.

"We'd better stop in the next town for Sunday school and church," Mother said.

"Oh, now, Mother, I don't think we need to do that today. We don't know where the Baptist church is, and we might have to hunt for it and waste time and . . ." Daddy ran out of excuses.

Mother did not argue, nor did she agree. Daddy whistled a soft little tune and kept the car rolling down the highway. In less than an hour we heard a loud *bang!* The car lurched and bumped along to the noisy *flap, flap, flap* of a very flat tire.

It was customary for the entire family to get out of the car and hover around Daddy while he fixed a flat tire. Proper conversation for the occasion was tender with sympathetic phrases, such as "What a shame," and "Now isn't that too bad," or "I wonder how it could have happened?"

To which Daddy might reply, "Some rascal probably threw a nail in the road." He changed the tire in somewhat the same manner a surgeon performs an operation. He stayed by the defective wheel, held out a hand, uttered a word or two, and expected the proper tool to be handed him with dispatch. No one was out of danger until the operation was completed.

That Sunday we had three flat tires. We never had that many in one day before—or since.

"Next Sunday, we'll stop for church, dad-gum-it!" said Daddy.

Daddy considered these trips across country very educational and told us to watch for interesting sights and notice the country we passed. He bought notebooks and pencils for each of us and told us to keep a diary as we went. "Your diaries will be valuable someday," he said. I wonder why we did not cooperate.

My diary went something like this:

July 16, 1927

4:30 A.M. We have left Altus.

5:30 A.M. We have crossed the river and gone through Snyder.

7:00 A.M. We have eaten breakfast. David got the most eggs.

11:00 A.M. We have gone through Oklahoma City.

12:30 P.M. We finally ate dinner.

6:30 P.M. We are in DeQueen, Arkansas for the night.

"That isn't what I meant," said Daddy. "Write about things that happen. Tell how beautiful the trees are getting."

It was true that every mile the trees were taller, more leafy, more numerous. Daddy eagerly awaited the mountains, but they came only after Nashville. Daddy loved his father and his brothers, but I think it was the land that kept pulling him back—a land he loved, full of boyhood memories; clear, cool springs of water; arching giant trees; and the hills, the mountains which sent him away and ever drew him back.

From Nashville to Cookeville and Algood was about ninety miles. Daddy could hardly keep his eyes on the road, and he needed to because it was endlessly winding its way through the mountains. Later, it was to become a part of the York highway.

"Alvin York lived across the hollow from us when we were boys," Daddy said. "His mother and my mother used to borrow sugar from each other."

The highway took us to Cookeville, where we had lived for three years, but we did not linger there. Another few miles and we were in front of Uncle Doc's house at Algood. Uncle Doc's house was the mansion of the family. It sat back from the street among the leafy sugar maples, its ample lawns stretching out in a luxury of space. The house itself was of red brick. The wide front porch overflowed with wooden tubs of flowering hydrangeas, behind which was a wide, comfortable porch swing where Grandpa Moore spent his thinking time. If we were very quiet, we could sit in the swing beside him, or even in his lap.

Since Uncle Doc's back porch was screened, it was there the family ate meals in the summertime. Between the back porch and the garage was a walk covered by a grape arbor. I liked the grapes best just before they were ripe, still tart and slightly green. "You'll get a bellyache for sure," said Grandpa when he saw me eating them. "Now just such a girl as that!"

Our part of the house was the sun parlor. The sun parlor with its walls of windows opened to the sun on the south and east. Big Auntie furnished it in rattan chairs and sofas. In one sunlit corner was a desk and chair, making it easy to write letters. At one end of the room was the radio. Its huge, bugle-like speaker rose from the top. Coming out from its side was the cord to which were attached Grandpa's ear phones.

In the evening, Grandpa clamped the head piece over his ears and tuned in his favorite programs. In this way, he also accomplished the delicate feat of tuning us out. Occasionally, Grandpa was asked to keep an eye on us grandchildren while our parents went to a party or on a coon hunt. "I don't mind watching David Franklin," said Grandpa, "but I can't do a thing with that Connie."

Grandpa never had the full care of us. Uncle Doc's house was always well supplied with help. So far as I know, Uncle Doc never turned away a patient, rich or poor, black or white. If the patients could not pay for his services with money, they gave their time and efforts. Someone was always working in the yard or in the house or keeping the children. Besides this, Big Auntie (so called, according to Daddy, because she had such a big, welcoming heart for the whole clan) had regular help. Her treasure, in our estimation, was Winnie.

Winnie was a tall, slender, intelligent Negro woman. She took orders from Big Auntie only. The rest of us took orders from Winnie. She served delicious meals at regular intervals, on time to the second. We learned to sit around the sides of the back porch so we were ready when Winnie served the table. Only Uncle Doc came and went at any hour. For him, Winnie and Big Auntie put aside food and kept it hot or cold until he returned from a call.

Afternoons, the men sat in the yard and talked. Sometimes they talked about old times. Daddy was the one who told the funniest stories. Uncle Doc said he exaggerated everything, but he liked them too. I always hoped Daddy would tell my favorite story about the time his galluses broke.

"That was the time I took a girl berry-picking," Daddy started off. "You remember Molly, don't you, Doc?"

"Oh, yes, I remember Molly," said Uncle Doc as he blew pipe smoke through his lips.

"Well, Molly and I were picking berries to a fare-you-well. It was a pretty spring day and I was jumping over bushes and showing off. Well, sir, once I jumped too hard and too long, and all of a sudden my galluses broke. I felt my pants going down over my knees. I tell you I broke and ran away so fast you couldn't see me for dust. I climbed the nearest tree and started hollering for help. I think it was Henry that found me and got me down. I never knew what became of Molly that day. I guess she ran all the way home."

Everybody laughed—even Uncle Doc, although he said, "I bet there isn't a word of truth to it. Just one of Marvin's stories."

He did not laugh when he and Daddy talked about heredity and environment. Uncle Doc tried to convince Daddy that any child would turn out right if he were given the right environment in which to grow up. Uncle Doc defended his position to the point of anger.

Daddy would have none of it. "Blood will tell," he said. When neither of them convinced the other, they talked of other things. They remembered a girl who lived in a poor family. In her late teens she was still unmarried. One day her father chided her about it.

"You going to live here all your life?" he asked. "What's the matter; won't no boy have you?"

"That girl married in a few days," said Uncle Doc sadly, knocking his pipe against the yard chair.

"And died from heartbreak and mistreatment in a few years," said Daddy. "I tell you, no girl of mine will ever get married till she's good and ready. I'm not trying to get rid of my children— not ever."

I should have listened to that story a lot closer than I did. If I had known what a deep impression it made on Daddy, I would have understood him better in my teen-age years.

There was always excitement and fun in Tennessee for us children. There were plenty of cousins to keep things lively. My favorite was Mary Catherine (or Cacky, for short) who was just my age. Two cousins, Margaret and Penock, were several years older than the rest of us, and we looked on them as special creations. Penock was tall, handsome, and straight as an arrow. He went to Culver Military Academy, and his manners were impeccable. He called Uncle Doc "Father" in a dignified way that made our "Daddy" sound downright hicky. Margaret we adored. She could do the Charleston, and also the black bottom—whatever that was. Mary Catherine said she could, so she could. Her hair was bobbed, shingled in the back, and feathered around her face.

One afternoon while Daddy was not around, she took the shears and bobbed my Buster Brown-type haircut even shorter and shingled it in the back. When Daddy arrived, there was a not very pleasant scene, but Margaret vowed I never looked so cute. And, anyhow, nothing could be done about it then.

Sometimes in the mornings, Margaret entranced Mary Catherine and me with an imaginary visit to fairyland. She took us around the dew damp lawn to where the elephant ears grew. Here, she told us, was the place the fairies came to play on nights when the moon was full. There were two fairy queens, she said. She looked at me. One was blond and always wore blue velvet robes trimmed in ermine. She looked at Mary Catherine. The other had dark hair. She wore gold velvet robes and sable furs.

Margaret's imagination was as boundless as our eagerness to hear the lovely tales she spun from it. Many a golden hour she held us spellbound as she told her never-never-land tales. I can remember nothing in my childhood more enjoyable than visiting fairyland with Margaret.

One trip we made to Tennessee was exceptional in every way. We stayed more than three days, and we made the trip with two other families, Uncle Holt's and Uncle Henry's, from Eldorado. Never before had we tried a three-car convoy of Moores, and I think no one in the family has ever considered trying it since. We had a family reunion in Tennessee, and then the Oklahoma Moores went to the World's Fair in Chicago.

What a time we had on the way! There were twelve people to please every night about tourist camps and eating places. It was

1933 and the summer was hot and dry. We put wet towels in the car windows to try to keep cool. I had just turned fifteen. That was the summer I had a crush on Penock. On this trip I kept a diary, and it was slightly more descriptive than the first one.

SATURDAY, JUNE 24: We're having a keen time. We are now in DeQueen, Arkansas for the night.

MONDAY, JUNE 26: Tennessee is gorgeous. We got to Nashville about noon. After supper I laid down on the sofa and almost went to sleep. Aunt Leila came and looked at me and said, "Isn't she beautiful!" I adore Aunt Leila.

TUESDAY, JUNE 27: In Algood at last. Gee, it looks beautiful. We've been swimming. Dad didn't say anything about my bathing suit—hotcha!

WEDNESDAY, JUNE 28: A marvelous day. Cacky and I went to Cookeville with Penock. Then Penock took just me and I really felt honored!!

Sunday, July 2: Went to Sunday school and church at Cookeville. All the kinfolks (29 or 30) had our pictures taken in the afternoon.

Thursday, July 6: Chicago!! We went to see Lake Michigan and are only about three blocks from it. We have lovely apartments but they cost our families $40 for five days. Phew!! Daddy nearly had a fit, but this is where the others wanted to stay.

FRIDAY, JULY 7: Oh, my poor feet! We have really been to the Fair. It's grand, it's marvelous, it's beyond human description and endurance, but its *the* World's Fair of 1933. I love it. We've been in most of the free exhibits, and the Chrysler and Oriental buildings are the most beautiful. Daddy wants to see everything that's free. He walks and walks. Uncle Holt got tired and sat down on a bench and told Daddy to go on walking all the way back to Oklahoma if he wanted to, but *he* was going to rest awhile.

SATURDAY, JULY 8: We went on the Skyride today—marvelous view but otherwise not so hot. Daddy said it was an awful waste of money and that we should spend our time looking at the educational exhibits. He liked it when I played on a Baldwin grand piano made especially for the World's Fair and costing $3,000.

MONDAY, JULY 10: What a day! We went shopping all morning, and I never saw so many people in my life. In the afternoon we went to the Chicago Theater, the most beautiful one I've ever seen. Show was grand. Then we went swimming in Lake Michigan. It's swell—and no salt!

WEDNESDAY, JULY 12: Well, we are back in Oklahoma, close to Tulsa for the night. Beer was voted "in" in this state yesterday. I don't know what to think. Uncle Henry says there are certainly two sides to the question. It's hot, but we're in our home state and feeling fine.

The summer I was seventeen, I went to Tennessee alone, by train. How many hours of discussion and prayer it may have taken for my parents to let me make the trip alone, I do not know. Daddy finally decided I would be perfectly safe if I wore his Masonic pin. "Any Mason who saw it anywhere in the world would see that no harm came to her," Daddy said.

I think Mother felt the experience would do me good. In another year I would be going to college, and I should be learning how to do many things on my own. At any rate, they let me go. My excitement knew no bounds.

JUNE 23, 1935: I'm on my way! I'm really going to Tennessee —unless, of course, Daddy changes his mind and has the train stopped at Snyder. I've got my window up as far as it will go. Things blow in my eyes, but I don't mind. Awhile ago, I changed my seat to one in the prettiest part of the train, but the conductor came in just now and asked me if I knew I was in the smoking car. I told him "no," and we found another seat. I'm so thrilled. It was grand of Roberta and William to come see me off.

We are now in Lawton and quite a few people are getting on. I finally put my window down and is everything dirty! I certainly am glad I put that little brush in.

JUNE 25: Penock met me at Cookeville and drove me to Algood.Then Cacky rushed me off to the Girl Scout Camp. Everything is so beautiful it hurts. I almost broke my neck trying to pick flowers on the bluff over the river but it was worth it. We went swimming in the Caney Fork and this afternoon hiked to the most beautiful swinging bridge I ever saw. I was on the list to cook supper; I cooked all the hamburgers.

JUNE 26: Penock came after Cacky and me this afternoon early because Grandfather died today. I'm so glad I talked to him before we went to camp. Dad is coming tomorrow.

Tennessee is beautiful tonight. Calm and clear and stars shining everywhere. I love it. At camp there was a beautiful hemlock tree.

JUNE 27: Dad is here and, oh, he hurts so much. About the first thing he asked me was if I had talked to Grandpa and if he recognized me. When I told him how I told Grandpa Daddy wanted to come see him, why Daddy just cried more. But I think it made him feel better—oh, I hope so. I haven't seen Dad like this before. He got a telegram from Brother Leazer and the deacons. It was so sweet, and Dad appreciated it so much. It's just like Brother Leazer to think of it. It helped Dad a lot.

JUNE 28: The funeral was sad. Daddy cried and touched Grandpa's cheek one more time. I wish he hadn't because it would feel dead and Grandpa will always be alive in our hearts. I comforted him the best I could, and I think it helped a little. I tried to take Mom's place, but no one could do that.

It was beautiful—the place they buried him—out in the country beside the little church. Now that it is all over, I believe Dad has improved 100 per cent. Pen said so too. All of them are trying to be more cheerful. I wish the others could have come --Daddy said they all wanted to.

JUNE 30: Daddy has gone. Rosa Lee took him to Nashville and he tried to hurry her, but we saw him cry—bless his heart. And, oh glory! He gave me $25 to take four piano lessons from Mr. Goodman at Nashville! Tomorrow morning at nine I have my tonsils taken out. Uncle Doc says to go to bed.

July 3: Here it is Wednesday, but I don't mind skipping over the last two days, because they were pretty painful—not the operation, but the aftereffects. The operation was fun because I couldn't feel anything, and I could see and understand what was going on. Uncle Doc was swell, and he said I was an unusual patient. My throat still hurts when I swallow, but I'm eating regular meals today.

July 6: Went to Nashville today with Cacky and Big Auntie. I paid $25 to Mr. Goodman and also bought a Debussey number I'm learning. My first lesson was worth the whole $25, and Mr. Goodman is all I hoped he would be. He is a short, plump, big nosed, white-haired little man and he has tiny, short, stubby fingers. He crosses his feet when he plays and pounds on the pedal with the foot underneath. He smokes big cigars and has the grandest Steinway in his studio, that Cacky and I take our lessons on, you ever saw.

The first thing I did was to play "Flight of the Bumble Bee." He had already found the music and made gestures to me during Cacky's lesson and I nodded back that, yes, it was mine. Well, I was quite nervous and played it awful. But I was very surprised when I got through to hear him say, "That was nice. You have good fingers and you play fast."

Then I played "Romance" for him. He liked it fairly well and played some of it himself. Well, I didn't like the way he played a chord, and (forgetting who he was) I told him so. He looked startled, and then I think he sort of liked it because he said if I came back and played it as he did, he wouldn't have any use for me. It was all very nice.

He said (after I had played all the pieces) that I had talent and temperament, and good interpretation. One time when I answered a question intelligently, he said, "Why, certainly, certainly. That girl can think."!! Oh my—I wish Daddy could have heard that. But in every piece he found wrong notes and a little bit of wrong time. He catches every mistake and marks them.

Mary Catherine said she never had so much fun in her life as listening to Mr. Goodman and me talking and playing. She and I listen to each other's lessons. That is just like taking two lessons. She told Big Auntie all about it, and Big Auntie said she reckoned Mr. Goodman and I would get along fine. I hope so.

JULY 7: Went to Sunday school and to church morning and night at the Methodist church here at Algood. They all stood up and repeated something about believing in the holy Catholic Church. I didn't repeat that part because, for one thing, I don't believe the Catholic Church is holy, and I didn't think the Methodists did either.

In Nashville I took my second lesson from Mr. Goodman. When he said I had improved and played better than last week, I liked him even more. He was so patient with me.

JULY 17: I practiced and was lazy (mostly lazy) today. Jack and I hunted cardinals, then climbed the magnolia trees, and whistled to them. They answered back. It was grand fun.

JULY 22: I took my third lesson and had loads of joy in doing it. Mr. Goodman was surprised at the way I'd improved on the third movement of Beethoven's *Moonlight Sonata*. We're invited to lunch and to go for a swim Friday after we take our piano lessons from Mr. Goodman at his summer home at Monteagle. I suppose we'll get to meet his wife and children too. We feel quite honored.

JULY 26: What a day! Last night Mr. Goodman called to say that he had to be in Nashville today and we'd have to come there instead of Monteagle. I wish I hadn't written everybody about it before it happened.

I smiled during Cacky's lesson when he played one of her pieces as I liked it. And he saw me and peeked up over his glasses and said, "Oh, do you like that?"

I said, "Yes, very much," and he smiled and looked so pleased!

"Well, fine—fine! She likes it!" he said as though he had made an important announcement.

After the lesson, Cacky went over to him (smoking a pipe today) to pay for her extra lesson, and he said, "I'll tell you what I'll do. I'll take just half of this if you'll spend the rest on *Oklahoma* there and have a good time." And he meant it! (Now we can go to Harriman, Tennessee, to visit Uncle Haskill and Aunt Maude. Cacky has a pass, and since it is $2.15 round trip I didn't want to write home for any more money. But we did want to go. Also went to see *Smilin' Thru'* with the rest of it.)

"Mr. Goodman," I said, "I wish you would come to Oklahoma and play for our high school assembly."

"How much will you give me?" he said.

"Nothing. Come for music's sake." Mary Catherine almost fainted. He convinced me he couldn't do that. I do so like him.

AUGUST 1: We went down to Aunt Sophia's for ice cream. It was yummy. I leave tomorrow. I'm glad and sad. July has been a grand vacation month. It has taught me things—mostly to appreciate home and the friends and things I have around me everyday. Also to be glad for nice Tennessee relatives.

AUGUST 8: Well, I've been home almost a week, but I suppose I should tell my dear vacation diary I got here just fine. All the family met me at Oklahoma City, and we kissed and hugged and kissed again. It was a lovely trip. Sometime, I think it would be interesting to travel by myself and see things and do things. I have written to everyone who entertained me—and I really meant it when I said I'd had a good time—it was swell, and the music was best of all. Everybody says I have improved. I'm still working on my pieces as hard as I can, which isn't so very much. Good old Tennessee rains—good old Oklahoma.

Of all our family excursions in the summertime, even counting the one to the Chicago Fair, to me none could compare with our trips to Galveston. Daddy had two loves in Texas. One was the city of Dallas, and the other was Galveston Bay.

Why Daddy felt so close to Dallas was something past my understanding. The most interesting thing about the place to me was the elevator in the First Baptist Church.

On Galveston trips we became familiar with two great churches, "Dr. Truett's church" and the First Baptist Church at Galveston. We found the Sunday school and B.Y.P.U. in the two churches similar to our own, and we felt at home as visitors. Something about the vast auditorium at Dallas and the solemn white-haired man who stood in its pulpit awed us to reverent pause. This was the man who never failed to pray for the boys away from home in the days when Daddy was a lonely, hungry boy sleeping under the banana trees in a Dallas park hundreds of miles from his native Tennessee. In this church he found friends. He had pictures of them on B.Y.P.U outings and Sunday school picnics.

"I owned a piece of property in the heart of Dallas at one time," Daddy said. "If I had kept it, it would have been worth a lot of money today."

Daddy had business to attend to in Dallas on the way to Galveston, so we knew to expect a stopover there. Sometimes we went to the park while he was downtown. The slides were higher, the swings went out farther, and the jungle-gyms were harder to climb than at any other park we knew. If we had not been on the way to Galveston, Dallas might have won our hearts too.

An even worse obstacle than Dallas was Houston. We never stayed there as long as we did in Dallas, but by that time we could almost smell the sea, and our impatience knew no bounds. Houston was undoubtedly the hottest place in the world. We sweltered in the car while Daddy made his business calls.

A few hours later, we crossed the causeway to Galveston Island, simply beside ourselves with excitement. "Oh, Daddy, please may we go swimming before we find a place to stay? Please? Please!"

"Could we just drive by the beach to look before we find a place to stay?"

"May we just go wading first for a few minutes?"

Finding a place to stay took time. Daddy would not stay in the gay, smart hotels and tourist courts close to the bay. He insisted they were far too expensive. He and Mother looked at place after place until they found a clean apartment not too far away from the beach, where Mother had a small kitchen to fix our meals. We certainly would not eat out.

Where or how we ate was the least of our childhood worries. But having to wait to get settled and buy groceries was torture.

Eventually, we were in our swim suits, covered with robes or towels or both. Old, patched innertubes were swinging on our arms, and we were on our way to the beach. If we were going for a short swim, we sometimes went to Stewart Beach with its wide expanse of sand beyond the sea wall. But the first whole morning at Galveston, Daddy took us far down the east beach or even to the west beach.

One morning, he took us in time to watch the sunrise over the water. We stood in the warm, damp sand and saw the world turn to a fantasy of pink glow like the inside of a clean conch shell. Everything was touched with pink—the sky, the sea, the sand, our faces, our hearts. In a moment, the pink changed to a golden-yellow glory reflected on every wave breaking at our feet. The sky matched our bedazzled eyes shining with the delight of such a beautiful morning.

Daddy showed us where to look for shells and how to recognize the unusual ones. On our walk, we came upon an old fisherman pulling in a net full of wiggling life.

Later in the day we went to watch the shrimp boats come in. "Why do they smell so?" I asked.

"They smell like fishing boats are supposed to smell," said Daddy. "They are as clean as can be. See, there is one being cleaned." He pointed to a small boat being scrubbed by two barefooted men.

"I don't think I like shrimp," Virginia said.

The big thrill of any trip to Galveston was a ride out into the bay on the good ship Galvez. The Galvez was a pleasure boat. It had a string band on board made up of white-coated, darkskinned musicians. To board her we paid for tickets at a stand where a man called through a megaphone, "Step right up, folks.

Get your tickets here. Boat leaves in exactly three minutes."

"Oh hurry, hurry, Daddy. We'll miss it!"

Daddy did not hurry. He haggled with the man until he obtained a family rate. We walked up the gang plank onto the boat. Mother found us seats together on the main deck.

"Let us go on the top deck, Mother, oh please let us." For years, Mother's "no" was firm. Finally, David and I were old enough to ride high above the water with only a railing between us and the sea. The boat churned through the channel to the bay while the band played loud and strong. Out in the bay, Daddy pointed to floating "cabbages" and seaweed.

"Look at the big fish!" we cried. There were indeed big fish following the boat. They slipped in and out of the water in graceful motion.

"Those are dolphin," said Daddy. "They follow the ship because they get food from it. They like to play. Now, if you watch, you'll see them playing follow the leader."

Out in the bay we saw big ships. "The U.S. Navy," said Daddy. "And those over there are shipping boats. Look at the flags they are flying. You can tell by the flags which country they come from."

Suddenly, we were out in the big waves. The Galvez lifted high toward the sky and plunged down into the sea. The wind whipped strong and damp across the bow. It blew my hair back from my forehead, and my dress clung to me like skin. I stood on the top deck and looked out across the sea to where it touched the sky. While the boat kept its stedfast course against the wind and waves, I felt a oneness with the earth. I was a part of the height and depth of the changing sea. I loved the exhiliration of the stiff wind and the plunge of the boat. Something of me went out to meet the vast secrets of the sky. I wished I could hold fast to the loveliness of this moment.

But it was only a moment. On the deck beneath me, people clung to their chairs and wished aloud for the smooth boredom of the narrow channel. As if the captain had known all along that his passengers preferred the shore line, he turned his ship in a wide arc and headed it back into the bay's calmer waters.

The string band played loudly. The slap, slap, slap of the bass fiddle kept it relentlessly in time. The rest of the trip was earthy. I pushed the sounds of music and pleasant conversation and Coke bottles as far out of my consciousness as I could. I held tightly to the feeling I had when the ship lifted high and plunged hard against the wind. It was a moment of joy which became a part of something more than my physical self.

Once, late in the evening, Daddy took me to the pier to watch the waves at night. The lights on the pier were bright and blinking. We turned our backs to them and stood silently, our elbows on the railing, watching the breakers foam on the shore.

"I love to watch the sea," I told Daddy.

"I love it, too," he said.

One morning, Galveston newspapers carried a warning that a hurricane was approaching. Mother began to pack our suitcases for immediate departure. Daddy started plans for leaving, but he was in no hurry. He took us for a drive around the city to see how people prepared for a storm. We were amazed to see men hammering huge boards across every window.

"That breaks the wind and keeps it from crushing the glass in," Daddy explained.

Before we left, he took us out to the sea wall. The sky was dark and the wind was high. The breakers swirled angrily against the sea wall. Daddy told us about the great tidal wave that hit the island in 1900.

"So many people were killed they never got the actual count," said Daddy. We shivered and held his hand.

Virginia leaned against Mother. "Let's go home," she said.

"That was before this sea wall was built," continued Daddy. "It couldn't happen again."

We stood on top of the huge wall. A wave cracked against it, sending wet salt spray on our faces.

"Don't you think we'd better go, Marvin?" Mother asked.

"Oh, there's plenty of time," Daddy answered. "The storm isn't due for hours yet."

My heart beat faster in a tight knot of fear, but I was fascinated by the furling white breakers and the piling waves hurling themselves against the sea wall.

"The ocean is beautiful," I breathed.

"I think so, too," said Daddy.

Yet the climax of any summer vacation was the satisfaction of getting home again. The house looked so clean; our rooms were prettier than we remembered.

I lost no time in reaching for the telephone. "Marguerite? Can you come over? We're home!"

5

Hold That Line

When I was thirteen, I fell in love. For quite a while, I kept my love a secret. Walking home from junior high, the girls talked about their boy friends.

"Connie hasn't got a fellow," they would say.

"Who wants one?" I would counter. I said that for days.

When finally I said defiantly, "I do, too!" they plied me with questions until I blushed.

"Who is he?"

"I'm not telling."

"What are his initials?"

"I can't tell or you'd know." This was absolutely true. His initials were as unique as the ones I shall use here—S. Q. His parents had the only name in town beginning with "Q," so initials were a dead giveaway.

"Is he in the seventh or eighth grade?"

"Neither."

"He's in high school! Freshman, sophomore, junior, senior?"

"I'm not going to tell." I couldn't either. Stanton Quarles was a senior. He was the student director of the junior high orchestra. Twice a week he spent an hour at junior high working with the small group of students who played one instrument or another. I was the piano accompanist.

"Oh, you're just kidding. You don't really have a fellow." But something must have made them doubt their doubts. "What's the matter, are you ashamed of him?"

Since I was very, very proud, I said not another word and walked home with my nose in the air.

I said nothing to Mother on the subject, but I had the feeling she knew. The Quarleses were members at First Church, and once in a while our families went on picnics together out to Red River. Mother probably understood why I took a renewed interest in GA work. Our GA counselor lived directly across the street from Stanton. If I sat in the chair next to the door, which was opened to the fresh spring air, I could see Stanton across the street hitting a tennis ball against his house.

I became a tennis enthusiast, which pleased Daddy very much. He and Mother had played tennis when they were young (ages ago), and he wanted us children to learn. He had recently bought some property in the next block from our house. He had the house moved away to another location. And with help from friends and neighbors, we cut the weeds, rolled the ground down hard, and chalked the lines for a tennis court. Daddy got some posts, huge ones, telephone posts, I think, at a good bargain; and they were put at either end of the court. For some reason the wire, which was to go over the posts for a backstop, never got up, and we spent most of our time chasing tennis balls.

One blissful Sunday evening, Brother George had the B.Y.P.U. general assembly elect a boy to lead the singing and a girl to play the piano. Stanton was elected singer, and I was chosen pianist! I remember how my hands trembled when I played the first chorus Stanton called for.

"Now everyone stand up and sing 'In the highways, in the hedges, I'll be somewhere a-working for my Lord.'"

The key was G major—my favorite key to play by ear. I launched into it and Stanton soon had the rafters ringing. When the chorus had its due, Stanton leaned over the piano and whispered, "Can you play 'Wide, Wide as the Ocean' without music?"

I could. It was in the key of C. I also did fairly well in E-flat major, and any hapless song played by me was usually put in those keys, whether that made it slightly higher or lower than it was supposed to be. Once in prayer meeting, I played "What a

Friend We Have in Jesus" in G, and only Mother even attempted to sing when we got to "Oh, what needless pain we bear."

These choruses had gone well. I heard Stanton bragging on me. "We're fortunate to have a girl who can play the choruses we learn at Falls Creek. Thank you so much, Miss Moore."

Everyone laughed at the Miss Moore part, but it was friendly laughter. It was not the first time good things had come my way because of piano playing; nor was it the last. Sunday mornings, I was pianist in the Intermediate department. William Reynolds led the singing. Since he was several months younger than I, I was not so much in awe of him, and we got along well.

My only problem was trying not to get a fit of giggles when he said something funny in an aside to me. He could go on leading a song looking solemn. "Let us sing number 39," he announced. While leaves of hymnals were fluttering, he leaned over the piano and said, "Bringing in the she's." This would fracture me, but he went on leading the song. And only I heard his particular rendition as he sang with angelic expression "We shall come rejoicing, bringing in the she's."

William was a good song leader. People said he was like his Uncle Ike, of whom he was very proud. When William's Uncle Ike came to visit from the seminary, we could tell he was somebody special, but everyone in the church said Brother George was still the one they liked the best.

Brother George asked me to play for Professor Reynolds, and I tried my very best to play so Brother George would be proud. Of course, I tried too hard and did worse than usual, but the tall, distinguished gentleman from the seminary was very kind. "You must come to Southwestern Seminary sometime," he said.

So ran the blessings from a knowledge of piano. It did not occur to me to tell Daddy, "Thank you for all the lessons you've let me take," or to think Mother's constant reminder and enforcement of practice had anything to do with meeting celebreties or having happy feelings in B.Y.P.U. assembly. I accepted without question what people said about my being unusually talented as the full explanation.

The secret was out about Stanton and me after that B.Y.P.U. assembly, though. "Stanton's robbing the cradle," they said.

I did not even think of having dates. I knew my parents would think I was too young, and I did not even ask. I saw Stanton at school, on the tennis court, at church, and at B.Y.P.U. socials.

There was many a B.Y.P.U. party at Roberta's house. Roberta was the only child of Brother and Mrs. Leazer, who came to live in the parsonage after Brother Burton went to another church. Since Roberta—or Bobby, as we usually called her—and I were almost the same age, we became fast friends. If there was a party at her house, I was sure I could go.

For some reason, my parents felt that nothing untoward could possibly happen at the parsonage. It is the only place I can remember being given carte blanche permission to attend a party from start to finish. I could even spend the night with Roberta when Mother felt it was really convenient with Mrs. Leazer and that it was not just a put up job between Roberta and me—mainly me.

The Leazers were Baylor graduates. Uncle Bob, as we came affectionately to call our pastor, was a football great while he was in college. Everyone leaned a little forward in their pews when he preached his sermon on "The Great Coach." Mrs. Leazer was a lady with the old South touch. Her house, even in the old parsonage, was charming and full of gracious ease in spite of the bustle all around it.

I felt important when I went home with Roberta for Sunday dinner. The Leazers had a maid who prepared the meal, served it, and cleaned the kitchen afterward. Even with me, chattering in quicksilver spurts during the spacious intervals between conversation at the table, theirs was a quiet, dignified mealtime compared to the five (or eight or twelve, depending on relatives and friends) Moores.

After Sunday dinner at Roberta's, she and I went to her room, and her parents went to theirs. "Maybe we can all have a restful nap," smiled Mrs. Leazer as we left.

"I certainly feel like one," said Brother Leazer.

When we were in our room, I asked Roberta, "Does your daddy really take a nap on Sunday afternoon?"

"Why sure he does," she answered, "doesn't yours?"

Of course my Daddy did. But he wasn't a preacher! He was only a deacon, and deacons just naturally took naps on Sunday afternoons. Preachers were different. At least, I thought they were. I thought they spent Sunday afternoons going out in the highways and hedges trying to win people to Christ. Except when they were praying for sick people or having a funeral or a wedding or—the more I thought about it, the more I wondered if maybe Brother Leazer might not need a nap like Daddy. I was disillusioned, though.

One warm summer night, all the Intermediates and young people came to a B.Y.P.U. party at Roberta's. Apparently, most other parents felt the same about the pastor's home as mine. I was to spend the night with Roberta after the party.

Everyone had a wonderful time. The social committee planned games and contests. We laughed at crossed questions and crooked answers. We collected forfeits and played "heavy, heavy hangs over your head." In order to regain his forfeit, Stanton was asked to tell which girl he liked best of all.

"Connie Bett," he said without even hesitating. Everybody laughed and started teasing me. I felt my face getting hot, and I pretended to be very embarrassed. But I was glad as glad could be.

The party ended with singing. Stanton led some choruses. He went from one to the other without stopping, and I had to watch carefully to keep up with his beat. Roberta's high clear soprano poured out the melody. Maxie blended an obligato above the rest of the singers. "In my heart there rings a melody," they sang.

Finally, Stanton started "Come into my heart Lord Jesus." Everyone sang it soft and low or swelled it out when Stanton directed them. It was a delight to sing when he directed the music. Stanton was dedicated to be a singer like Brother George.

When we finished singing "Into my heart," Brother Leazer led in prayer, and the party was officially over. As couples left or were picked up by parents, we sang some more. Stanton did not lead now. He sat beside me on the piano bench and sang tenor to "Let Me Call You Sweetheart." Everyone wanted to sing "Shine on Harvest Moon" two or three times before they left.

Stanton, Roberta, and I went out on the front porch. We sat in the porch swing in the cool darkness and swung lazily back and forth. There was a slight squeek in the chain attached to the porch ceiling, but who noticed things like that?

Roberta's mother called her, and she went inside a minute. Stanton put his arm along the back of the swing behind me. His fingers touched my shoulder. He bent his head and whispered in my ear, "You're sweet."

I can still remember the dress I wore. It was pink batiste in a flower print. It had a sash, tied in back with a bow, a white organdy collar, and it was sleeveless. At Stanton's words, the night changed from silvery darkness to soft pink, and the porch swing floated off into space somewhere like a pink and gold morning on Galveston Bay. Only I was not on the shore this time. I was closer to the top of the highest ray of gold the sun sent up into the blue sky.

Roberta came back to the swing. Stanton went in the house to thank Mrs. Leazer for the party. He said "good night" to Roberta and me and went home.

"I'm going to marry Stanton," I told Mother one bright June morning.

"Oh," said Mother in a mildly interested tone. Years later, she told me her heart stood still for a moment. "Let's see, you've just had your fourteenth birthday. Don't you think this is a little too soon for marriage?"

"Oh, Mother, I mean I'm going to marry him when I do get married. I want to get engaged on a moonlight night in June when I'm eighteen. And then on June the fifteenth, when I'm twenty-one, I want to marry Stanton."

"June fifteenth, when you are twenty-one," mused Mother. "That is seven years from now, 1939, if my arithmetic is correct. When did you and Stanton decide these things?"

"Mother!" I exclaimed. "You don't think Stanton knows about this—I mean about the *when* part. It's just that I love him, and I know he loves me. So someday we'll get married. And isn't it the girl who decides when she'll say 'yes' and when she will marry?"

"Connie Betty," said Mother as kindly as she could, "what you have is a good case of puppy love. You are too young yet to know what real love is."

That is what everybody said. I was too young to know what love was; Stanton was robbing the cradle; it was puppy love. I grew to hate the words. I knew I loved Stanton, and I was sure he loved me. He gave me his senior class ring to wear. I put tape around it so it would stay on my finger. On Christmas, he gave me a white gold lavaliere with what looked to be a diamond in the center. Stanton said it positively was not a diamond, but Mother said she did not think I should accept a gift of jewelry. Much to my surprise, Daddy came to my rescue: "Oh, I think it would be all right for her to keep it, Mother."

In January, the Quarleses moved to another state, and Stanton entered the university there. I cried all evening after he left. I tuned the radio to a station where the orchestra was playing "Lover Come Back to Me" and cried even more. Daddy made me turn off the radio and asked Mother what in the world was wrong with me. When Mother told him, he said, "Oh, she must have more sense than that!"

My parents, although they missed their friends, must have felt a certain amount of relief at the way events had transpired. They were forewarned of what was coming. They knew that, by whatever name they might call it, a new dimension was added to my life. I had left childhood behind and found growing up to be a delightsome land.

So my parents, knowing my eagerness and my vulnerability, drew up a line for my protection and well-being. I resented it, of course, because to me it seemed a fence to keep me from fun and freedom. I had no capacity for realizing that to them the line was a velvet case where jewels are kept until lifted by appreciative hands to a place which best shows their splendor.

The line was a set of rules and regulations, all of them unwritten, and many of them unspoken. Almost without exception, they came from the teaching and preaching of Southern Baptists.

Every evangelist who preached our August revival had sermons on the sins of this generation. At one service during the meeting, the men only were invited to attend. After that service, the ladies eagerly listened to what their husbands told them the evangelist said. By the time I had a husband, such meetings were not held where I happened to be, so to this day I do not know what they were about.

There was plenty I did hear in the regular services. The cardinal sins were these: drinking, dancing, card playing, mixed swimming, movies, and smoking—in that order. None of these sins sent you to hell. Only unbelief in Christ could do that. It was that by not doing these things one lived the Christian life.

There was unanimous agreement concerning the evil of beverage alcohol. The day of the open saloon was still fresh in the memory of many people. I know of no lady among Mother's acquaintances who was not a member of the W.C.T.U. So far as I know, Daddy never took a drink of liquor in his life.

At least once a year in junior high assembly, we heard a speaker from the W.C.T.U. One lady I remember in particular. She showed the usual charts and pictures as we sat in the gymnasium. When she began her speech, she became quite eloquent. "She's preaching," someone whispered.

Since I was definitely on her side, I tried to ignore the "preaching" remark. But she talked louder and louder, using her hands and arms in wide gestures. As she spoke she moved backward step-by-step. When she backed into the blackboard which held the charts, she stopped, walked a ways up the gym, and began again. About the third time she backed into the charts, there was muffled laughter. We had been listening for a long time, and it was hard to keep still.

When the pledge cards were handed out, I signed my name to promise I would never drink beverage alcohol. I also resolved that I would not become a member of the W.C.T.U.

In spite of unattractive proclaimers of the facts, the facts themselves stood. It made sense to me to avoid absolutely something which, even in the smallest amounts, could disparage normal physical processes and which in large and constant dosage could end in living death.

There was never any question in my mind as to whether I would go to dances. My parents said I positively could not, and that was that. There were, however, many questions in my mind as to *why* I could not.

I stood on our front porch one evening and watched the two daughters of our neighbor leave for a dance. Their pastel dresses swished and folded in graceful fulness as they went away. Their father was a deacon in our church, too.

"Why do they get to dance?" I asked.

"I don't know," said Mother. "But I do know they are not the kind of girl I want you to be. Even if every girl in the whole town does something we consider wrong, it doesn't mean you need to do it."

Then Mother bought yards and yards of net and made me a formal that took my breath away. The net was off-white, and to go under it, Mother made a silk slip of soft green. For a sash, Mother got wide, pale-green, velvet ribbon to tie in a bow on the back and hang to the floor. There were ruffled-net short sleeves, and the skirt was wider at the hem than any dress in Altus that year. I wore it to the annual junior-senior banquet one May night when I was asked to sing on the program. I sang "Somebody Loves You." I loved to sing. It was easy, and it was fun.

The junior-senior dance was after the banquet. I hardly gave it a thought. Singing while wearing Mother's creation left nothing to be desired.

The next year, I had a dress of lavender organdy, and Mother always said it was her favorite dress for me. My sophomore year, the banquet theme was Spanish, so Mother dyed the off-white net bright red. She added black-net ruffles to the full skirt and made a black bolero that laced in front. At the dime store, I found some black-loop earbobs and for one night wore them!

The sophomores traditionally served the banquet. I can never remember having more fun at Altus High than I did that night in the gym. I served the Board of Education table and another table where only boys sat. They helped me serve their table by stacking plates and by other outrageous manners. One of the boys sent me a corsage of sunburst roses tied with a gold ribbon, and each of the other boys kept pretending to be the sender. They teased me and told me I was the prettiest girl there.

Mother and Daddy were at the Board of Education table. The sedateness of their table was quite a contrast to the riotous table of boys, and I could not help overhearing them tell Mother and Daddy nice things.

"You made it yourself?" one of the ladies asked Mother.

"You didn't really dye that net! And the slip too? My, my, but it does look lovely, and so appropriate for a Spanish banquet."

"How about hiring out as a maid at our house, Connie Betty?" one of the Board members asked me.

They all laughed, and Daddy said, "We can't get this much work out of her at home."

That evening I had the deliriously heady sensation of feeling like a belle. If one can feel that way, does it matter whether it is belle of the ball or belle of the banquet? I wonder if Mother purposely outdid herself on those dresses in hopes of creating just such a situation. Or did she do it because she could not do otherwise with her heart full of love for her children?

The spring I was a senior, my dress was heaven-blue chiffon. Mother said it was the hardest to make of any, and she almost decided to give up sewing after that. It was fitted in the front and shirred to a flowing fulness in the back. The back bodice had overpanels that floated softly when a breeze caught at them. It was a sleeveless dress, and under it Mother put a white-taffeta slip with tiny ruffles at the hem. She also made my full length, white-satin, hooded cape, which stood me in good stead all through college. Daddy never said a word about how much our clothes cost as long as Mother made them.

The formals were not for just one occasion. They were for

piano recitals and parties. But they meant the most on the nights they stood among those of girls who went to the dances. They made the grade, and, truthfully, I never felt I missed very much.

Dancing was the great divide at high school. It was a far greater divide than whether or not you were a church member, or even whether you were a Christian. The majority of high school students danced; a very few did not. Most of the Baptist young people danced. If you danced, you had the chance of being "in," of being included in all kinds of parties and groups. If you did not dance, your social life was restricted to church functions and a few home parties for the same church group. At our house, these parties were given as often and as lavishly as my imagination requested, and they included friends who danced. But the wall was between us.

Those of us who did not dance considered ourselves consecrated Christians. We never thought of actually calling the other young church members "unconsecrated Christians," but we certainly thought of them as different. It seemed to me they considered themselves socially superior because they danced. I did not feel a whit socially inferior to them, but it never once occurred to me that any one of them might feel not a whit less consecrated a Christian than I! I heard no preaching or teaching to open my eyes or heart to understand that Christians could disagree on how they lived their Christianity and still be Christians. Summer evangelists never spoke of humility or pride in their sermons on the dance.

The modern dance, they preached, was an almost certain prelude to unchastity, immorality, even adultery. It was especially hard for boys to keep their emotions under control after a dance, and no girl could be sure she would be safely escorted home after such an evening.

Daddy stood with the preachers against the dance. He was not alone in his agreement with them. There were others, but most of them were not the crusader Daddy was. While Daddy was on the School Board, there were no dances in the high school gymnasium. The board was not composed of Baptists only, nor even a majority of them. Banning the dance in the gym took a majority vote, but I have no doubt that it was Daddy who convinced them.

Why were the preachers so adamant in their denunciation of the dance? Why did Daddy feel that it was so very wrong?

In Uncle Doc's autobiography, I found some answers to why Daddy felt the way he did. Here is Uncle Doc's description of the dance as he and Daddy knew it in their Tennessee boyhood: "Social functions were very limited in these days. They had no orderly dances. Church people opposed dancing and parents would not allow their daughters to attend them. So dances in the neighborhood during my early boyhood were rowdy affairs and not participated in by the best class of young ladies. These were drunken brawls lasting sometimes two or three days and nights at a time. They often ended up by fights and bloodshed among the young men. This situation deprived the young people of this era of what might have been a harmless source of fine physical exercise and great enjoyment."

When Uncle Doc's children were teen-agers, the Tennessee culture in which they lived included what Uncle Doc approved of as an orderly dance, and he allowed his children to attend them. But Daddy left the mountains and came west into the lusty, hard life of the frontiersman. The West of those early days knew dancing as a part of the saloon and the red-light district. Daddy's soul revolted at anything connected with such degradation, as did the clean-hearted, clear-tongued preachers of the new West. By the time I was a teen-ager, dancing was inextricably connected, in Daddy's thinking, to all that would be harmful to a daughter. And loving his daughters more than life itself, he let us know he would go to any length to protect us from such harm. So he absolutely forbade the dance.

Not only were playing cards never seen in our house, but also we were not allowed to have a Pollyanna game because dice were used as counters. I learned this fascinating game at a neighbor's house and played it there. Our house had rules.

Uncle Doc's book also helps explain the way Daddy and others like him thought of card playing: "Here I make a statement I don't think could be made about any area of its size in the whole United States today. When I was a boy, I am sure you could not find a deck of playing cards in a single home in the Calf Killer Valley. They were called gambling cards which should not be allowed in a home. Gamblers and playing cards were something we heard about but never saw. Church services were not only religious gatherings but were also to a great degree social affairs before and after church. People traveled for many miles in wagons, buggies, and horseback to attend a big church service. Great church revivals lasted from one to four weeks, the preacher appealing to nonchurch members to come to the mourner's bench to pray for forgiveness of their sins. . . . They were the foundation and beginning of the leading churches of today. They contributed freely to funds for foreign missions."

I do not know that Uncle Doc intended any inference between his first statements about there being no playing cards in the valley and his last statement, "They contributed freely to funds for foreign missions," but perhaps the connection was a stronger one than any of the good mountain folk or their Western sons realized. Card playing was connected with gambling, a monster which was known to deprive children of food and women of proper care. Even if one had money to burn, however, here was the spark to kindle into fire: foreign missions!

Because a needy world beckoned, Altus Baptists frowned on any game played for prizes—much less, money. Money spent on such trivial things was wasted, for there was a place it was needed. Mother and the other ladies of the WMS felt they would be slackers if they spent an afternoon at a bridge table when they could have spent the time quilting and giving what was earned by those thousands of tiny stitches to foreign missions.

Preaching about mixed swimming came with the advent in the West of civilized public swimming pools. Nothing in Daddy's background prepared him for this, and, acting like a thoroughbred Baptist, he balked. There were no cement pools in the Calf Killer Valley, but there were plenty of streams and rivers. In vain did a well-educated, city-bred deacon friend explain to Daddy that if the Lord meant us to swim, he would have put scales on our bodies. In Daddy's boyhood there were times when he had to swim if he got across a stream. And how anyone could prevent mixed swimming on Galveston beach staggered Daddy's imagination. Besides, Daddy knew some preachers with different views. He was with them, and their families were with his family, at church picnics (before anyone even thought of a city swimming pool) when everybody swam in the river.

Nevertheless, Daddy kept a firm eye on our behavior in the water. When we went swimming, *we swam.* He expected Mother to see that we were decently clad at all times, but he took into consideration that in order to swim, certain concessions had to be made to practicability.

Since I was undersized anyhow, I am sure I got by with more daring swimsuits than I would have had otherwise. There was a red, wool one with the neck and shoulder straps trimmed in diagonal red and white stripes and a matching belt. Mother let that one pass, but she was not with me in Tennessee the summer Uncle Haskill had some samples of rubber swimming suits which were all the rage that year. I tried out a two-piece, pale-pink one when we went for a swim in the Tennessee River. I think it was the color more than anything else that made the other swimmers turn startled glances in my direction. I did not wear it again.

My favorite swim suit was a one-piece, navy wool proudly bearing a badge declaring me to be a Junior Red Cross Lifesaver. As a campfire girl, I worked hard for that badge, and Daddy and Mother both bragged about it. "Now, that's something really worthwhile," Daddy said.

Movies were quite another matter. I am sure I shed quarts of tears over not being allowed to go to movies. Daddy was harder on the movies than any preacher I can now remember. He read disapprovingly of the "goings-on" in Hollywood. The films had too much dancing, too few clothes (Movie stars did not wear swimming suits to swim in, according to Daddy.), and there was entirely too much love-making. Daddy had a strong conviction that a steady diet of movies was detrimental to young minds.

Besides all this, taking the whole family to a movie was too expensive. "Why, we could buy a croquet set and play every evening the whole summer for what it costs to go to one movie," exclaimed Daddy. Circus tickets once a year were one thing; a movie every two or three weeks was just "too much of a good thing."

Mother subscribed to *Parents' Magazine,* and an approval of a movie on their page of reviews was my best chance of attending one. Seeing *David Copperfield* was a tremendous experience. *Smilin' Thru'* became a part of my idea of what real love was. *Sally* with its golden, sparkling colors opened a new world. *Peter Pan* delighted me. The whole neighborhood pretended to be parts of this story for years.

There were exceptions. David had influence I knew not of. How else did I get to see *Dr. Fu Man Chu* and *King Kong?* I had nightmares for weeks afterwards. It was David, too, who got me to the Saturday serials. I worried from one Saturday to the next how the cowboy would get the heroine out of the burning house. In spite of exceptions and *Parents' Magazine,* there was always restraint when it came to movies. They were bits of candy after meals, never a steady diet.

The problem of smoking was rather unimportant at our house. I never knew Daddy to use tobacco in any form, but he told us he smoked cigarettes as a young man. Or was it cigars? Anyhow, he decided it was a foolish, wasteful habit and cured himself of it. The cure had something to do with pepper, but I cannot remember what it was. (He had a cure for corns, too. He simply struck a match and set the corn on fire. He let it burn as long as he could stand it while he hopped around on one foot. He highly recommended the method to Mother, but she never in all this world tried it.)

Many of the men among our friends and relatives smoked, and Daddy never acted as though it was sinful. He simply made us feel that men would be far better off without it.

For women to smoke was different. I got the impression that

this was indeed sinful. It was supposedly more harmful to their health than to men. There was a vague question in my mind as to whether this argument was valid, but I never gave it much thought. I decided I definitely would never smoke because the habit seemed unfeminine to me. In the movies, ladies looked strange with puffs of smoke coming out of their mouths. Once, I noticed the yellowed teeth of an otherwise lovely girl. Looking pretty was a hard enough job at best. I could see no reason to make it more difficult.

So in our family, the line drawn by the church on the sins of this generation was pretty much the rule. I was to find, however, that my parents had other rules never preached at First Baptist. When I began to have dates, Daddy always wanted to know who the boy was.

"Who are his parents?" Daddy asked. "Do we know them? Do we know someone who does know them?"

"Oh, he's a very nice boy," I answered. "He's in my American history class."

"Every boy in Altus has to be in that American history class sometime or other" was Daddy's reply. "What church does he go to? What does his father do?"

"Well, he isn't rich or anything like that," I answered hotly.

"No one cares whether his father is rich or poor," Daddy's explanation was just as boiling. "But I'm dead sure not going to let my daughter go out with someone who doesn't come from a family that is decent and honest."

To Daddy, a good name was "rather to be chosen than great riches." He believed it took some length of time to make a good name. The fact that a good name was often accompanied by a certain amount of this world's goods probably had not escaped Daddy's notice. But when the testing time came, it was character and not riches that was Daddy's measuring stick.

Underneath all his thinking lay Daddy's concern, almost a fear, that someone might think he did not want to keep his family intact as long as he could. Perhaps there were fathers in the Calf Killer Valley who, of necessity, had to push their daughters into unwanted marriages. Daddy knew no such necessity. It was unthinkable in the past; in the future even the appearance of such evil was to be avoided. His daughters would have to be sought, wanted, and asked for. Did he envision them as the charming young ladies of Dallas in First Baptist's B.Y.P.U.— young ladies whose company he could enjoy at B.Y.P.U. picnics, but into whose homes he found invitations hard come by? And did he, instead of resenting it, appreciate it and respect the heads of those homes because they represented what he wanted to be? Dallas, its First Baptist Church, and the preaching in his own home church were the standards Daddy held high. They had shown him what he wanted. He intended his family to live up to those standards.

One Sunday afternoon in midsummer, I went to a meeting in the main auditorium of Altus First Church to talk about Falls Creek. Falls Creek! To Oklahoma Baptist young people the words were as magic as any in the English language. Ten days of heaven-on-earth! Heaven-on-earth in very earthly circumstances! Although Altus had one of the best cabins at the encampment, there was no running water, no bath facilities, and, to tell the truth, the roof leaked. Cooking was done on an old iron stove by ladies of the church, who came to do hard labor-of-love for the ten days so the young people could be free to go to classes and meetings.

"If just one young person finds the Lord's will for his life, it will be worth it all," the ladies would say. Mother was one, of course, and there was Mrs. Dobbs and Mrs. Haralson and others whose names I cannot recall.

Once we found a very young couple to chaperon the group, but Daddy immediately stated I could not go. "It takes more than just being married to make a chaperon who can take care of young people for ten days," he said.

I was very put out with him, but finally we found chaperons of whom every parent approved. "But we couldn't have done it if it hadn't been for Brother George," they said.

Brother George went every year. He was the headman, the

handy man, general flunky, gatherer-of-supplies, keeper-of-the rules, dish dryer, wood gatherer, fixer-of-the-leaky-roof, and official chaperon of the boys who slept on cots outside the house or in the kitchen. Somehow, Brother George also managed to teach classes and help lead the singing at the encampment. He kept reminding us that we were at Falls Creek for a purpose. And he kept checking up to be sure we were attending classes.

Oh, it was such a glorious time for us! The morning began on the mountaintop with sunrise devotions. Who was that girl—such a lovely girl—who played the violin and told us in soft clear words what the Lord Christ meant to her?

After breakfast, we hurried over to B. B.'s music class. Then came Hot Dog's B.Y.P.U. hour. In front of our parents we called them Mr. McKinney and Mr. Lee. But since they were not ordinary mortals, we had special names and special places in our hearts for them.

Having been brought up by Brother George, most of us filed into the choir loft for the morning worship hour. When B. B. stretched out his long arms to start the singing, it seemed as though the whole world would respond.

> Jesus never fails,
> Jesus never fails;
> Heav'n and earth may pass away
> But Jesus never fails.

We sang, oh, how we sang! Lee Baum played the piano. He played all over the piano. We watched in awe. He had a handkerchief tied around his head. William Reynolds put a handkerchief around his head, too.

Brother Farmer made announcements. He gave figures telling how many were registered at Falls Creek. "If we keep on growing," he said, "we're going to be bigger than Ridgecrest."

We sang some more and settled back on the benches to listen to the morning speaker. Once, it was Dr. Holcomb from First Church, Oklahoma City. One year Dr. Dana, from Southwestern

Seminary, had the morning worship hour. Every morning, he spoke on prayer. A listening, yearning part of me strained to catch every word. Dr. Dana made prayer a living, vibrant way to God's own presence.

In the afternoons, we took long hikes and went swimming. A few hardy souls played tennis in the hot summer sun. Sometimes I went alone for a walk up the hills around the encampment. I did not go very far. There was a tree I liked which had a low limb just right to sit on. I leaned back and looked at the sky. I liked to sit there and talk to God. "I love you, dear God," I said. "I wish I could do something for you."

I wondered how it would be to dedicate my life to foreign missions. I was sure I would be a missionary if God called me, but I did not feel that he had.

One day I read from the twenty-eighth chapter of Job: "There is a path which no fowl knoweth, and which the vulture's eye hath not seen: . . . He cutteth out rivers among the rocks; and His eye seeth every precious thing." "There is a path"—for *me*, my heart cried out. It did not have to be a path like anyone else's; it did not even have to make sense to anyone else. The only important thing was that his eye would see it. It was his path I wanted to take. I did not care where in the world it might lead.

At the evening services at Falls Creek, we heard many famous preachers. The one I remember most vividly was Dr. R. G. Lee from Memphis. "Let me see your hands," he called out one evening. We held them up. How many there were and how alive they were! "Now look at them," said Dr. Lee, "and think how God gave you those marvelous instruments to use for him." He told us about a lake inside our ear and made us feel we had something priceless, something infinitely precious, to give to God.

Toward the end of the encampment, an invitation was given to those who wanted to dedicate their lives to Christ. With pounding heart, I made my way to the front. I was not the only one who came. The aisles were filled with young people. William Reynolds came to dedicate his life to Christ in the field of church music. There was much rejoicing over William's decision. The Reynolds were greatly loved.

"Are you dedicating your life for any special field of service?" I was asked when I reached the front.

"No," I floundered, trying to think what I should say, "just for anything."

"For anything God leads you to be?" I nodded. That was what I meant. I was glad to be understood. I stood in the long line with the others at the front of the auditorium while our reasons for coming were read.

"Connie Betty Moore, Altus First Church, life dedication." The words sent color surging into my face. I was glad I came to the front. Something inside me was at peace. But I was almost ashamed that I could not say where my path would lead me.

The Sunday night after Falls Creek, those of us who went to the encampment gave our report of the ten days' events to the evening congregation in our home church. When my turn came, I was trembling. I tried to say something funny about how the roof leaked. There was enough gentle, sympathetic laughter to give me courage to try to explain the wonderfully joyous experience of hearing the whole camp singing one afternoon as the rain stopped. "The sun came out," I told them, "and it made the clean, wet trees look so very green. Over the top of the hills we could see a rainbow. Then we could hear people singing all over the encampment. House after house sang B. B.'s song:

> 'He sends the rainbow, a lovely rainbow;
>   He sends the rainbow with the rain.'
> He sends the sunshine above the shadow,
>   He sends the rainbow with the rain.

It was so beautiful. At Falls Creek, everything makes you think of God and love him more."

I swallowed something in my throat and plunged ahead. "And while I was there I went down to the front and dedicated my life to Christ. I don't know what he wants with my life, but whatever it is, that is what I want to do for him." I felt tears stinging my eyelids. I meant to say it so much better than that!

"Amen," I heard a deacon say softly. When I sat down, I glanced at my parents. Mother smiled at me and Daddy cleared his throat loudly.

After the service, I was unprepared for the warmth and kindness of the congregation. People spoke to me and said, "God bless you, we'll pray for you," and acted as though they were proud! No one seemed to mind that I could not explain everything of how I felt. They seemed to understand! I have never forgotten how my church family helped me that night. To this day, their smiles and love are a lift to my soul.

In my zeal to serve Christ, I longed to do anything I possibly could to show that my life was his. I resolved to obey my parents. That did not mean I would not argue with them when we had a difference of opinion. But if I could not get their consent for something, I would not disobey them. This I would do for Christ's sake, because I felt it was what he wanted me to do.

Testing time for this decision came soon and often thereafter. Almost anytime I visited another girl for an afternoon or went to practice a program at school in the evening, someone put a record on the victrola or played the piano and everyone danced. "Come on, Connie, we'll teach you how," someone invited me. But I managed to have something else I needed to do at the moment. If they asked me why I would not dance, I tried to answer truthfully: "My parents do not want me too."

"They don't need to know about it. Come on, it's fun!"

"I don't think I should," I replied, and turned away. A part of me felt consecrated and peaceful, and another part of me wished they would like me and understand. Mostly they just left me alone, and they were not unkind about it.

One afternoon, I was in the home of a girl whose parents were friends of Mother and Daddy. Because she was older, had been to college, and had lots of boy friends, I told her secrets I shared with no one else. She even knew how I felt about Stanton.

Her cousin from out of town was visiting. Eventually, they

put a record on the victrola. The cousin asked me to dance, and I started my routine answer. The cousin listened politely, but suddenly my friend cut in, "Well, I haven't got religion that bad. And, thank goodness, I'm not engaged to a singer!" She laughed, but her words were like a knife.

"I'm *not* engaged to a singer," I cried. "That has nothing to do with it!" Both of them laughed and said they were only teasing, but I could tell they really believed I was refusing to dance because my boyfriend was going to be a church singer. They did not think I was doing it for Christ at all—they did not even think I was doing something of my own choosing!

That settled it. I would not marry a church singer. And I would certainly never marry a preacher! I would positively not marry anyone connected with church work. While I was thinking about such things, I decided I would not marry a doctor, either. Uncle Doc worked at any hour and sometimes all night. I would marry a lawyer who made lots of money like Judge Austin.

Daddy took me with him one evening when he went to see Judge Austin's office suite in the new, five-story Gosslin Building. Judge Austin was a deacon in First Baptist, and he greeted Daddy cordially. "How good of you to come visiting, Brother Moore! Hello, Connie Betty! Well, how do you like it? Sit down, Brother Moore, sit in that chair beside the desk."

Daddy, exclaiming at the fine features of the office, sat in the chair. Judge Austin held out his hand. "That will be five dollars."

Daddy jumped out of the chair, and the two men laughed loud and long about the cost of sitting in a chair in the new office. I did not laugh. I was too busy looking at the beautiful new office. I thought it should cost five dollars to sit in that chair.

If I married anyone, it would be a lawyer. But more than likely I would marry no one. I would be a missionary after all and go out alone to some faraway place. No one could say I was doing it for anyone except Christ. I did not bother to pray about this. It was so perfectly reasonable and right, I put it on like a piece of armor. And its hardness felt good.

My conscience did not bother me until the next year at Falls Creek. Then I began to remember that I vowed I would do *anything* for Christ's sake. As the days progressed, I began to realize that my friends were not the ones who mattered. Some of them would never believe my motives came from a desire to live for Christ. I must not let them turn me to another path.

"Dear Lord," I prayed silently in the auditorium while the speaker's voice rose and fell, "I will even marry a preacher if you ever want me to." At the moment, it was the supreme sacrifice. It would be even harder than being married to a singer.

The invitation that night was for those who wanted to dedicate their lives to full-time service, those who wanted to become Christians, and those who would rededicate their lives. Or if there were anyone who was "following the Lord afar off" and wanted to walk closer to him, they should come to the front.

I hesitated. I had certainly not *un*dedicated my life. But I was holding back on what I was willing to do. I did want to walk closer to Christ. People were coming down the aisles. Perhaps I should go too.

"Don't stand in the way of others," the speaker urged. "Your coming will make it easier for someone else to come."

I thought of those in our Altus House. If I went to the front, they would know I wanted to walk closer to the Lord, and maybe it would help them make decisions.

I made my way to the front. There was no high exultation in my heart. This was what seemed to be my duty.

The only description to fit my coming down the aisle that night appeared to be "rededication." I could not say I came "because I am willing to marry a preacher"!

I found there were others from our house who came down the aisle after I did, and they told me they would not have come if I had not gone first. But in the days that followed I sometimes felt they wanted me to tell them also *why* they came down the aisle.

Eventually, I came to feel that going down the aisle for rededication was not the best way to discipline myself. There might suddenly appear on my path another problem I had not thought of. When it came, I believed God would help me with it, and by his grace I would keep on going just the same. I made no more public decisions, but Falls Creek remained an unshakable blessing to my life.

A poem in my English literature book gave me an idea which was to have more effect on my life than I ever imagined when I was fourteen. The poem was Thomas Campion's "Cherry-Ripe."

There is a garden in her face
   Where roses and white lilies blow;
A heavenly paradise is that place,
   Wherein all pleasant fruits do flow:
      There cherries grow which none may buy
      Till 'Cherry-ripe' themselves do cry.

Those cherries fairly do enclose
   Of orient pearl a double row,
Which when her lovely laughter shows,
   They look like rose-buds fill'd with snow;
      Yet them nor peer nor prince can buy
      Till 'Cherry-ripe' themselves do cry.

Her eyes like angels watch them still;
   Her brows like bended bows do stand,
Threat'ning with piercing frowns to kill
   All that attempt with eye or hand
      Those sacred cherries to come nigh,
      Till 'Cherry-ripe' themselves do cry.

All the teaching and preaching I received led me to believe every girl's love was something to be desired and sought for. The poem's thought that lips were sacred and that a kiss was something to be kept and guarded until the right time appealed tremendously to me. I decided to be like the girl in "Cherry-Ripe" —well, maybe not as beautiful as she must have been, but no one ever made me feel that beauty was more than skin deep.

Any girl's love was something she could guard and keep for the one boy to whom it would be given. Until "Cherry-Ripe" time, I would give my lips to no boy. I resolved that the first time they were kissed would be when I promised to be a man's wife. Who would my financé be? Where was he now? It made life very exciting to be waiting for him and to keep something that would be his alone.

As my teen-age years came and went, I was completely unaware of the many problems I never had to face because of this one firm line I chose to draw. I kept my own secret, cherry-ripe ideal without much difficulty. I found, to my surprise, that boys had high ideals of their own. They seemed to want a girl to have strict standards if they were the same for one boy as another.

Keeping my resolve to obey the rules my parents drew up for me was not a job well done. Time after time, I rebelled at the thought of some of them. I argued, I said things no good daughter would say, I pouted, I sulked, I acted high and mighty, I wrote in my diary "I hate my Daddy" and scratched it out so there was only a dark blot left. And, what must have been hardest of all for my parents, I hurt and I wept when I could not understand why they refused to let me have my way.

I do not even now agree with all my parents' decisions. But I rise up to honor them for doing what parents seldom accomplish: They cared enough for me to think and plan for my best. They drew up a line of high ideals for my protection and happiness. And in spite of the opinions of others, their own uncertainty, and even my tears, they held the line.

6

Ah, Sweet Mystery
of Life

"Mother," I asked wistfully, not just once but many times, "how do you know when you're really in love—how can you be sure?"

"You will know," Mother assured me. The way she said it sounded as if there were nothing to worry about.

I began to wonder about real love. Nothing could shake my belief that I had been in love, but I kept finding myself thinking of it in the past tense. And I knew the real kind lasted. I found myself more interested in boys than in any one boy.

September, 1932, was still hot and very dry. Everyone wished it would rain. I was fourteen, and I entered the very new, up-to-the-minute-modern Altus High School. Football fever was catching, and there was many a high-spirited pep meeting.

Daddy was a member of the School Board. Everything about the school system interested him, and he was proud to be a part of it. Perhaps the depression assisted in causing the caliber of teaching to be far above average. Only the best survived in any job, and teaching was no exception. At any rate, I stepped into a high school blessed with excellent teachers. It is likely no coincidence that my favorites were the ones Daddy held in highest esteem.

There was petite Mrs. Fuller, the typing teacher. The click of keys in her room was as precise and clean as her white collar and cuffs. All Mrs. Fuller asked was perfection. Until that was attained, we kept aiming for it.

Every pupil in Latin class liked to have Mrs. Cotton walk past his desk. She smelled of lilacs, rain-fresh lilacs in the moonlight even. When we asked her what perfume it was, she told us and held her dainty handkerchief for us to sniff. But none of us ever accomplished the same degree of sweetness even if we tried the perfume. It remained Mrs. Cotton's alone.

Mrs. Cotton had short, white hair. Her glasses hung on a gold chain. She pulled them up and clamped them on her nose as she taught. Besides Latin, she instructed us in first year English literature. Who can forget her teaching of *Julius Caesar?*

Then there was Mrs. Peterson. In all the classes I was privileged to attend—high school, college, university, or seminary—I never found her peer as a teacher. In Mrs. Peterson was a spark of something as rare as the combination of harmless doves and wise serpents. You saw it in the twinkle of her eye and felt it in the tone of her voice. She cared more about how a pupil responded than she did his responses, although she meticulously graded the responses. She was the strictest disciplinarian in the school, but from her classes came more snatches of gay laughter than from any other. All she taught became special and alive.

Mrs. Peterson is best known, I suppose, for her debate coaching. The proof positive of that is her many championship teams. But that proof is needed only by those who have not been in her speech classes. Such pupils need only the miracle of what can happen to anyone who is guided by her notations on a slip of paper handed to each pupil after his speech was finished. She helped us see ourselves as others saw us and taught us how to be what we wished others to see.

To my way of thinking, Mrs. Peterson's greatest contribution was her senior literature and grammar class. Lord Byron, Keats, and Shelley became, not assignments on the pages of a book, but poets who wrote lines of shimmering beauty. After Mrs. Peterson taught us a poem, we went home quickly to read it aloud and

memorize the best parts. We learned to appreciate Oliver Gold-
smith, who "polished his couplets until they shown," and we discovered mighty Shakespeare's sonnets.

When we entered Mrs. Peterson's room, we invariably glanced
at the blackboard. She usually had a poem on the board, one she
thought we would enjoy. Often they were verses from the
"Cheerful Cherub" or something of Carl Sandburg's. This led to
our watching for poems in our mothers' magazines. I was not
the only one who bought a small notebook and carefully wrote
on the first page "A Notebook of Poetry." In it I copied the
poems from the board, pasted in the ones I found, or even wrote
one of my own!

Mrs. Peterson encouraged us. Since she was always saying
things I wanted to remember, I often wrote them in the margin
of my English literature book. "You will be busier and have
more to do every year of your life," she told us, "but you will be
only as happy as you are right now."

Mrs. Peterson, who was twenty-something, looked so pretty
standing in that sunny classroom. She had dimples and soft curly
hair. She was not slender; she was what Mother called pleasingly
plump. Our favorite dress for her to wear was one a shade-deeper
blue than her eyes with a white angora collar. We discovered
it was Mr. Peterson's favorite too.

"Come see me when I'm ninety years old," said Mrs. Peterson.
"I'll be on the sofa reading all the new magazines and books I
can find, and I'll be having the time of my life."

Of course, I spent no time appreciating my teachers while I
was actually in Altus High! The really exciting part of high
school was the social part—the extracurricular activities, and
especially the boys. I began to keep a diary in January of my
freshman year. In it, I wrote the really important things that
happened—things in which my parents seemed totally disin-
terested. Daddy especially did not want to hear anything from
me about boy friends. In my teen-age mind, he became a very
old-fashioned father who did not understand my generation at
all. He was too strict. And the worst of it was that Mother stuck

with him in everything. Nobody had such rules and regulations as I did—nobody! I told my diary all about it.

SUNDAY, JANUARY 1, 1933: A new year and it came on Sunday. I'm going to try harder to be the girl I should be, even if sometimes it isn't what I want to be.

THURSDAY, JANUARY 5: Well, David and I were scuffling today and broke a window in the kitchen. We both wanted the same hamburger—the biggest one. If Mother would only have hamburgers more often—but no, she only has what Daddy wants to eat (steak and potatoes and gravy, all the time). So we only get good stuff when he's out of town.

FRIDAY, JANUARY 6: I went to the basketball game and had a lovely time. We won. Among those present (ahem!) were: Ben, Charles, Pierce, Stroud, Marvin, and a few others. Daddy took me, so (of course) none of the boys came around. They're scared to death of him, and no wonder—he glares at them.

SATURDAY, JANUARY 7: "Why can't I have dates?" I ask. Daddy says, "Too young"—which means, of course, "You haven't got enough sense." I wish Mother would quit going around the house singing "I must tell Jesus all of my trials."

SUNDAY, JANUARY 8: For days, I have been waiting and saving so I can see *Tess of the Storm Country*, and tonight Dad informs me I cannot go. All the other girls are going. Oh why, why, is he like that?

TUESDAY, JANUARY 10: This afternoon Ben called me up for a date, but since Mother did not know him, of course she would not let me go. She had dates when she was fifteen, so I don't see why I can't when I'm fourteen. I cried, but it did no good. I can't have any fun.

MONDAY, FEBRUARY 6: Everyone I talk to about it thinks I have sense enough to have dates. Even Olen told me she didn't see why not. Tomorrow, we (my family and I) will have war over it!

TUESDAY, FEBRUARY 7: It wasn't much of a war. Mother didn't say anything and Daddy said NO! I ran up to my room and have been crying all evening. I guess I'm an awfully bad girl but I can't help but think he's wrong—wrong—wrong. I cannot feel the same.

FRIDAY, FEBRUARY 17: I just got back from the basketball tournament. I learned that last night Bennie and some more kids blew the siren whistle on the fire truck and they took Ben to jail! Don't know what to think.

On Friday, March 3, I invited Bennie, James, Maxie and her fellow and Roberta up to my house for Sunday. It was only when Daddy found out Roberta was coming that he said it was all right. I asked Ben to tell me what happened about the fire truck, and he did. I could hardly believe him. He said that he had nothing to do with it, that he was just there when it happened.

SUNDAY, MARCH 5: Well everybody came—the family was nice —the boys behaved excellent, and we had a grand time—just friends. Our revival started today.

MONDAY, MARCH 6: Uncle Bryan is here! I was singing "Sweethearts Forever" for him when Daddy came in and thought he was a boyfriend! He glared like everything until he saw who it was; then he laughed. Uncle and I went to church and they were worse than Daddy. Oh, I love to shock people who are so shockable!!

SUNDAY, MARCH 12: I don't understand life, but all I can do is try and just keep on smiling through. No one really likes me and I think it's because I don't dance. I guess this is my "Trail of Tears," like the Oklahoma Indians.

WEDNESDAY, MARCH 22: Bennie walked home with me, and later (he was at play practice) he called me. After while, Mother made me hang up, but before he did he said something like *ego amo te.*

FRIDAY, MARCH 31: Three months ago today, Stanton left, and tonight I cried all evening, except when I went to a Sunday school party.

We went to Sayre April 7 for music contests, and Altus won third place. We got firsts in violin solo, tenor solo, orchestra, girls quartette, and second in trombone solo. As far as we were concerned, that's all we could have asked for.

SATURDAY, APRIL 8: A pretty bad day. Mother caught cold at Sayre, both of us are tired and sleepy, and Dad came home feeling mad as the dickens. (This is to you and you only, dear diary, but it's true.) He wants me to be in the contests and he wants Mother to go with me (why I know not), but he doesn't want us to be away either. It's so beautiful tonight—clear with a big moon and delicate leaves shining. I love the spring, I do.

SUNDAY, APRIL 16: Easter Sunday—a beautiful day. No boy (tonight) can I think of who thrills me. Oh well.

MONDAY, APRIL 17: If the darkest hour is just before the dawn, the sun is certainly going to shine for me. Ben wanted to take me to a party, and Mother said NO! That's about three times straight, and Ben is probably out with somebody else. Can you blame him? She didn't give any reasons except the same old things—they don't know the people where the party is, and I'm too young anyway. Five years from now Virginia will be fourteen, and I'd almost be willing to bet that she'll be going anywhere she wants to (April 17, 1938).

WEDNESDAY, APRIL 19: Well, I'm going to write what I've been wanting to for a long time: Mother pets David. Anybody with one eye could see that anything he does is all right—but me, oh, that's different!

FRIDAY, APRIL 28: Altus debaters won first in the state contest today and will go to the national. That's grand!

MONDAY, MAY 1: I'm entering in English at the county contest this week—working hard.

SATURDAY, MAY 6: Bum day. I didn't get anything in English. I think maybe I spent too much time praying that I'd win.

TUESDAY, MAY 9: Our debaters are one of four teams left in the national tournament. Oh, *they've got to win.* I think and pray they will.

The Altus debaters were one of two teams left in the national debater's contest for the whole nation by May 10. The next day they broadcast over N.B.C. All in Altus were listening and backing them. Daddy and I sent them a telegram.

THURSDAY, MAY 11: Our debators won!!! National champions!!! The whole school went wild. We had a special assembly to listen to the last debate over the radio. Roy and W. C. were the speakers. Daddy and mother went over to the Dobbs's house to congratulate them about W. C.

SATURDAY, MAY 13: There is going to be a parade for the debaters (Mrs. Peterson, Roy, Marjorie, W. C. and Francis) when they get home. I'm going to sing at a banquet for them Monday night. I have a new, blue-taffeta dress for the banquet.

MONDAY, MAY 15: The debaters got home. We had a parade and everything! Oh! Boy! Then I went to the banquet and sang. It was fun. Daddy was there too, of course, and made a speech about how proud the School Board was. The debaters are so nice. I wonder . . .

TUESDAY, MAY 23: We went to the demonstration debate tonight and Francis smiled at me—oh, so nicely!

FRIDAY, MAY 26: I'm fifteen and what a day! What an evening! It's twelve now. Olen gave me a party and it was swell. W. C. wanted to take me!! But I had begged Mother, and she let Ben take me down to Olen's, but she brought me back home. Oh, I'm so happy, I'm afraid I'll wake up and find it's all a dream. I love Olen and Mom.

WEDNESDAY, MAY 31: The last day of May, the last day of spring, and the first day of vacation. Nothing is happening around here. I guess I'll get a good tan—rest up and be ready for anything and everything.

SATURDAY, JUNE 10: I think we are going to Tennessee as soon as the dentist finishes with my teeth.

TUESDAY, JUNE 20: My bridges haven't come in (for my teeth). I'm disgusted. Sez me. And how!

WEDNESDAY, JUNE 21: First real day of summer and the longest day of the year. We're leaving for Tennessee Sunday morning. Only half of my bridgework is in. Going without the rest.

By Monday my teeth were all straightened. Dr. Mary finished up on them, and I finally looked like a human being. Daddy acted like it cost too much and went into a bad mood.

TUESDAY, JULY 25: I went swimming at 6:00 A.M. and took some junior lifesaving instructions. It was grand. I'm going in the morning too. The campfire girls and boy scouts go to Lake Altus tomorrow. Mother is one of the chaperones.

WEDNESDAY, JULY 26: We're at camp. I kept guard from 10:30 to 11:00 P.M. The college boy who is assistant scoutmaster jumped out from behind a bush and scared me. Then he told me he liked me a lot and tried to kiss me. I pushed his head away and told him I hated him. It was like a nightmare. I know he had it all planned. He said so. Everything else was O.K.

THURSDAY, JULY 27: Mother was watching all the time last night while I kept guard, and she saw everything! She said she was proud of me!! I asked why she hadn't said something, and she said because I took care of the situation just fine. Can you imagine Mother saying that??? Honestly, you never know!!!

FRIDAY, JULY 28: I take the junior lifesaving test tomorrow. Here's hoping.

SATURDAY, JULY 29: And I did! I was the only one who passed it—and I had to pass it under Mr. Flemming!! I like him now. In one carry, I had to pull him out by the hair. Ah, sweet revenge!

SUNDAY, SEPTEMBER 3: I spent the day by myself. Nobody came, went, or wanted me for anything. I don't know what's the matter with me. Nobody loves me but Jesus, and I don't deserve him.

My diary further hints at the impact made on the whole town by the national debate championship. Everyone was debate conscious. Mrs. Peterson's speech class was an elective, but the

line before her door was already forming. I am sure there was
no place in town where enthusiasm ran higher than at our
house. In his connection with the school system, Daddy felt an
immense pride in something he considered so worthwhile. He
treasured an autographed picture of the four debaters and Mrs.
Peterson.

You can imagine the consternation of the School Board when,
in the midst of all this adulation, Mrs. Peterson resigned. Her
reason was as cheerful as it was simple. She loved her husband
and wanted to be with him. He taught in a community a few
miles from Altus. Mrs. Peterson planned to teach there too.

In very short order, Mr. Peterson received an invitation to
become the principal of Washington Ward School. It was doubtless a promotion for him, and in the middle of the depression, it
was unthinkable that he would refuse such an offer. But Mr.
Peterson said he could not accept the position.

"I just can't figure the fellow out," said Daddy. "I asked him
to come over here and talk to me about it."

The afternoon Mr. Peterson came, Daddy met him on the
front porch. I walked around the driveway from the back of
the house and stood where I could get a glimpse of Mr. Peterson.
I was dying to see him. He was tall, broad shouldered, and he
looked straight at Daddy, smiling as he answered Daddy's
questions without a moment's hesitation.

"I just don't want a job given me because people want my
wife to teach here, Mr. Moore," he said. "I do appreciate your
kindness to her and I don't blame you a bit, but I have a job
on my own and that's the only kind I want."

Oh, I thought, he is just right. Even for Mrs. Peterson, he is
just right.

Daddy was not smiling. His voice was concerned—he was almost begging! "Now, young man," he said, "don't you know we've
checked up on you and got references to tell us you are quali-
fied? We really need you here." Daddy talked on and on, and
I went back in the house before I was discovered and disgraced.

Mr. Peterson was principal of Washington Ward School that

September. Later he became high school principal and then superintendent of schools, strictly and definitely on his own. The Petersons were Daddy's pride and joy—and the town's!

I took good care of Daddy's autographed picture of the debaters and Mrs. Peterson. Roy and Marjorie Henry were cousins. Daddy said intelligence ran high in the whole family.

W. C. was the only one of the four who was a Baptist. He lived the next house down from Dr. Mary. Her office was in her home, and when I sat in the chair, I could see out the window to W. C.'s front porch.

All the girls swooned over Francis, who was conceded to be the best looking of the debaters. I was no exception. It was W. C., however, who asked me for a date at the beginning of the football season and thus skyrocketed my standing with the whole school. In this blissful moment of high school popularity, I was to be crowned queen of the debate carnival in October, an event I had not dared hope for in my starriest dream. Best of all, my parents approved of a boy, and I was allowed to have dates with him. Daddy called him "young Dobbs," as fitted one with a good family name. It was my happiest high school year.

MONDAY, SEPTEMBER 4: School has begun. I am determined to like all my teachers and just as determined they shall like me. I sat by Francis in Latin class. A grand day. Dad and I went to see Mr. Flemming, who is in the hospital. The freshmen are terrible.

WEDNESDAY, SEPTEMBER 6: I thought I made a failure in speech class and got mad and bit my pencil so hard I cracked my bridge and ruined it. Daddy nearly had a fit when Dr. Mary said I'd have to have a new one. When (later) W. C. told me I made a swell talk, I turned up my nose. This evening Mrs. Peterson said I made a good talk, and W. C. really *had* thought so because he said I made the best one! She told me not to get scared when I'm giving a speech. Act accordingly, Miss Moore!

FRIDAY, SEPTEMBER 8: Debate not so good. W. C. said I had the best constructed speech made. Mrs. Peterson said I had a good English lesson. I was bad in history class. I am going to grow up.

TUESDAY, SEPTEMBER 12: Debate no good today. I answered more questions in Latin than Francis. I haven't got any fellow nor any hopes for one in time for the ball game.

I decided I had been conceited and much else, but from then on I was going to be nice to everyone. I began to make a daily list of the wrong things I did and resolved to try not to do them again.

WEDNESDAY, SEPTEMBER 20: W. C. walked home with me, and I think he likes me. This morning a boy hit me with a paper wad and James told him if he ever bothered me again, he would make him eat the rubber band and like it!! I was so thrilled!

The next night, W. C. went to choir practice and Maxie had a party afterward. I was invited but since I was going to the football game with W. C. the next night, I only got to stay thirty minutes. W. C. had asked me that day, and I was excited when the folks said I could.

FRIDAY, SEPTEMBER 22: W. C. and I went to the football game, and he said he liked me—especially the way I smiled all the time! You never know! He's swell. I like him. Mom likes him, too. Daddy even talks to him!

THURSDAY, SEPTEMBER 28: The day started fine. Mom said I could go to the ballgame with W. C. But a while ago (about 10:00 P.M.) W. C. called on the phone and was mother mad! *They* probably go to sleep at a decent hour—*this* family goes to bed with the chickens.

THURSDAY, OCTOBER 12: We had the special assembly today and it was grand. After I sang my solo, I had to sing an encore. I think everybody liked it.

FRIDAY, OCTOBER 13: I was elected queen of the sophomore class this morning! Now I am up for carnival queen against four other candidates from high school and junior college. I was never so thrilled in all my life. I must be dreaming. And people called Friday the 13th unlucky!

SATURDAY, OCTOBER 14: There have been kids at my house all day making posters for the sophomore queen. They made some elegant ones. Oh, I can't help hoping I'll win. It's elegant to be queen, but its hard too, because you don't know what to say and you have to be so careful.

MONDAY, OCTOBER 16: At noon W. C. and I usually sit in assembly and talk. But this noon I was completely surrounded by campaign managers. When the bell rang, Casey came to my locker to talk. Casey is going to crown the winning queen. Oh, I hope I win—for more reasons than a million.

TUESDAY, OCTOBER 17: Oh, if I could only win. I must, but I'm afraid I won't. We went to the grainhouse to sell Daddy some tickets and tried to get him to buy a lot. But he would only get what he usually would. He said what satisfaction would it be if I won just because he bought a gob of tickets from his own daughter?

WEDNESDAY, OCTOBER 18: I'm supposed to be ahead in the queen's race, but I'm afraid the seniors are holding out on us. Oh, I want to win so bad I don't know what to do. But if I lose I'm just going to grin and bear it. We decorated a float tonight for the parade tomorrow. Will I win? Can I win? I must! I can't. Or will I??

FRIDAY, OCTOBER 19: I WON!! A victory for the sophomores!! And we beat them by 1,500 votes. Oh, I'm so happy I don't know what to do. W. C. took me to the carnival. He got us some confetti and we threw it on people and they threw it on us. Oh, I never had such fun! I thank thee, Lord.

Well, W. C. and I went to the football game, and on the way a man ran into us. It punctured one of W. C.'s tires and only bent the other man's fender. I told Mother but I did not know what Daddy would say, or what W. C.'s dad and mom would say. And what is more, Vernon beat us 7-6.

SATURDAY, OCTOBER 28: Nothing has happened about last night. W. C. said his folks told him to keep his mind on what he was doing. Which he *always* does.

MONDAY, DECEMBER 4: Debate and more debate! I'm working with W. C. on the affirmative. I can't believe Mrs. Peterson is letting me do it because anybody can see I'm not good enough to debate with W. C. But it's a grand feeling—I've got to do it.

WEDNESDAY, DECEMBER 13: The debate is over. I was terrible —but it's just me. W. C. and I debate Bill and Marjorie tomorrow night.

THURSDAY, DECEMBER 14: I did a little better in debate—I think.

SATURDAY, DECEMBER 16: Another debate. We were to divide up teams with Cowdan, and then their coach decided he wanted to hear a debate between two of us and two of his— before everybody! Mrs. Peterson picked W. C. and me to debate them! And I had a five minute rebuttal!

SUNDAY, DECEMBER 31: The year is ended. I've had lots of fun, but I'm afraid I haven't really done anything that's worth much. We watched the old year leave and the New Year come in at the church tonight, and when the whistles blew, we prayed.

When the second semester began, W. C. dropped debate, which did not make Mrs. Peterson very happy, to put it mildly. He said he liked debate, but he always planned to do some other things and he could not do them all at the same time. He had a fine baritone voice, and there is an April entry in my diary saying, "W. C. won his voice contest." He did not leave debate for good, however, because later he was on the team at Baylor University.

WEDNESDAY, JANUARY 17, 1934: W. C. talked to Mrs. Peterson and everything's O.K. as far as friendship is concerned. When I took my music lesson, Mrs. Putman cried because I spent so much time on debate. Isn't everything crazy? Why couldn't I have been the one to stop debate and W. C. the one to keep on? Then our teachers wouldn't be unhappy, and everything would be all right.

WEDNESDAY, JANUARY 31: Well, I have a part in the one-act play "Enter the Hero"—not the best part. I'm Ruth. It means I'll have to stop debate. Mom said "one or the other." I love acting, and I'm not very good in debate anyhow, so it's O.K.

So the debate fever subsided. Mrs. Peterson kept on polishing her speech students, and her debaters kept on winning tournaments. I imagine she was relieved to have things get at least partially back to normal.

Daddy was not too pleased with this turn of events. Debate was one thing; dramatics was quite another. However, even Mrs. Peterson told him I was gifted in that direction, and what Mrs. Peterson said carried weight with my parents. The rest of my high school days were filled with the contests that were so popular at the time—contests in dramatics, tennis, typing, music —contests in everything. I tried them all! A beautiful Indian girl beat me in the city tennis finals. I received a letter A for placing second in district piano. Oddly enough, the highest award I received in all this competition was a second place in state for typing!

My best friend became Jon—Jon Scott, I shall call him. Jon was a "preacher boy" in our church, a personable high school senior, who played a lot of tennis. Daddy could say nothing against him. He knew his parents and they were friends. Daddy never said he did not want a daughter of his to marry a preacher. But did he think being a preacher's wife was fine for some women but not for his daughter? He never said.

FRIDAY, FEBRUARY 2: Mom and I went to Tipton tonight to hear Brother Leazer preach at a revival. Jon Scott was there too. Brother Leazer said something about Jon's going to be a preacher and my being a missionary maybe, and somebody in the choir asked when we were going to get married! They didn't know us, of course! Jon goes around with Jan and Jane and those kids, and he used to go to dances. So no one believes he's really going to be a preacher.

SATURDAY, FEBRUARY 3: Jon Scott preaches his first sermon tomorrow for youth night at our church. I'm so scared for him I don't know what to do. All the kids are praying for him.

SUNDAY, FEBRUARY 4: The service is over and Jon covered himself with glory. He looked elegant in the pulpit preaching. His eyes (brown) are so sincere. We all prayed together in the study before the service started. Daddy didn't like that at all. He said he never heard of Brother Leazer having ladies come in his study to pray for him before he preached. Oh, sometimes Daddy is so awful.

One Friday night Jon got the car, and the diary records the following weekend:

"He likes me better than any girl he's ever gone with—he said so. I like him. I want to see a lot of Jon, and he wants to see a lot of me, or so he says.

"Somebody told me they heard Jon say he found the girl he'd been looking for at last. Bill phoned and said Jon told him one of the minor reasons he liked me was because I didn't neck, and it had to be a swell girl that could resist the technique(??) he tried on me. All he tried to do was hold my hand as any boy does. I wouldn't let him because I knew he didn't really want to—he just wanted to see if he could.

"Jane said Jon said I was his dream girl and he didn't know one even existed. I don't believe it. I wish it was true though."

Everyone seemed to like the idea of a preacher boy dating a girl who might be a missionary. I did not like that idea, but I liked Jon. I tried to ignore the smiling nods-of-approval and the way people seemed almost to push us toward each other. I would rather have told them than have them tell me how nice it was. Because it was.

WEDNESDAY, FEBRUARY 14: Valentine's Day! And Jon sent me flowers! They are simply beautiful, and I was so thrilled! Tonight he took me to prayer meeting and held my hand when the lights went out for the baptismal service.

MONDAY, MARCH 5: Spring is almost here. I went skating with Nella Faye and Florence this afternoon. I asked Mrs. Peterson about Jon's coming to my locker all the time, and she said it was all right if we weren't tardy to any class and made good grades.

FRIDAY, MARCH 16: We're at Alva for the play contests. We started early this morning. The play got third, and I got third in acting for girls—a pretty long way from first. Pretty discouraged.

TUESDAY, MARCH 20: Play practice and was it bum!! I was the worst one. Jon came after me and took me to choir practice. He just got his senior ring and it's a honey. He told me he wished to wear it a week and then I could have it—as if I wanted the old thing! I do!

THURSDAY, MARCH 22: Weelll—I don't know exactly what to say. I wore Stanton's senior ring all day—and Jon acts funny . . . .

SUNDAY, APRIL 1: I spent Easter evening with Jon. He offered me his class ring as a token of his love, but I wouldn't take it that way. Besides, I did not think he really wanted me to have it. He sent me the loveliest Easter corsage that I have ever seen—sweet peas and roses.

MONDAY, APRIL 2: I was kind of blue today, and Jon thought it was because of what he said yesterday about my being a butterfly. Now he wants me to be. Really, it's because I want to wear his ring, but I won't because I don't believe he wants me to.

TUESDAY, APRIL 3: I have Jon's senior ring! He put it on my finger. It fit fine—he said he knew it would!?

SATURDAY, APRIL 7: We're home from the district contest at Weatherford. The play didn't win, but I got first place in acting.

MONDAY, APRIL 9: A nice day. Beautiful weather! The city contests are tomorrow. I'm entering in piano. Jon had a tennis match. I told him if he beat it and the next one, he could have a date. He beat this afternoon.

TUESDAY, APRIL 10: I won the piano contest, and now I am to go to the county contest. Jon won his tennis match, Jinna won her contest, and David's glee club won.

But the biggest surprise was in the paper. On the front page was a piece about me winning in the play contest at Weatherford, and it said the judges said I had "more dramatic talent than anyone found in this section of the county in years." I was thrilled, naturally, but I thought they should have said more about the others. When I said so, Mother and Daddy acted as if I did not appreciate the paper.

SATURDAY, APRIL 28: There's a full moon tonight and I want somebody—I don't know who. Mom says I haven't even met my Prince Charming yet, and I suppose she's right. I had a keen time playing tennis this afternoon.

TUESDAY, MAY 1: I'm in the high school National Honor Society and so is Jon. I think we're both going to get watches. Jon was mentioned as one of the best students of the senior class. I'm awfully proud of him.

FRIDAY, JUNE 1: For "what is so rare as a day in June"? This has been one of those rare, almost perfect days. Jon came down this afternoon, and we had lots of fun. Only Daddy came home early, and I don't think he likes for Jon to be at the house so much.

SUNDAY, JUNE 17: We took Grandpa over to Eldorado right after Sunday school and stayed until now, and I am very sleepy. Jon was licensed as a preacher at church tonight. And I missed it—I'm crying. He's going to have a revival meeting in a little country church pretty soon.

MONDAY, JULY 23: Mother, I, and Jon's mother went to the little church tonight. Jon preached a good sermon, and two people were converted. He was so happy he cried. It was a strange feeling to see how much he cared.

WEDNESDAY, AUGUST 1: Jon wanted to take me to prayer meeting—but Mother said "no." She gave no reason. I suppose grownups shouldn't give *children* any reasons.

"You are seeing too much of each other," Mother said. But that was not a reason to my way of thinking.

When school opened in September, Jon enrolled in Altus Junior College, which was conducted in the high school building. We saw each other every day, and we were quite exclusive in our companionship. Jon believed he was in love. I knew (and my parents kept helping me remember it) I had two years of high school and four years of college before me. It was not time for me to fall in love. Jon was my best friend, and any time I had the choice, I shared my thoughts and time in his presence. It was spiritually uplifting, mentally stimulating, and just plain fun to be with him. I loved him dearly as a friend, but I refused to let it be the real kind of love.

I cannot say my last two years at high school were happy and carefree. There were spots of happiness in them, but the weeks were punctuated by quarreling and making up with Jon. I was constantly aware that people felt we were together too much.

I wish now I had not worried so much. Jon and I never parked or necked. The most popular place for such things was on the drive around the city reservoir. One night, Jon and I decided we would drive around the lake just to see how many cars were parked there. On the narrow turn onto the drive, we missed the little sideless bridge with one back wheel and went into the ditch. Jon called his father, who stoically came and pulled the car back on the drive. We never tried the road again except in respectable daylight.

During my junior year, I began to have the trouble with my voice which has plagued me from that day forward. It began with laryngitis, caused by what? Too much cheerleading at Falls Creek when I was a campaign manager for our candidates for king and queen? Singing too high and too loud in the choir even though Brother George cautioned me not to? Frustration from trying to please everyone and myself at the same time? At any rate, I developed a halting speech pattern, sometimes barely discernible, sometimes powerful enough to make speech utterly unattractive and almost impossible, and sometimes entirely disappearing long enough to make me think it was gone for good.

My parents took me to a throat specialist, who assured them

there was nothing physically at fault with either my vocal chords or my throat. Probably the trouble would soon go away.

SATURDAY, OCTOBER 6: I thought my voice was a little better until I went to the party tonight and talked too much. Maybe this will be a blessing in disguise if I can learn to just not talk. But, oh, it's so awful. . . . At my piano lesson, Mrs. Putman said people were saying Jon and I were going to get married soon. Of course, it's perfectly silly, and it makes me so mad.

MONDAY, OCTOBER 22: Mother and I had another argument. I talked to Mrs. Peterson, and she said Mom was the most charming and intelligent person she ever met and that she knew best. So I told Jon, and we are going to try not being together so much. Oh, what's the use of being good if people talk anyway?

TUESDAY, DECEMBER 11: I'm crying and I'm down in the dumps. Why shouldn't I be: I have nothing to look forward to on this earth. Mother and Dad and every older person talk about how the best part of your life is your high school and college days—and when you're married you're married for a long, long time. And I'm nothing but trouble to them—all the time—never pleasing them. And when I do try to please them, Jon and I fuss. If marriage is so awful (And I'm not having such fun now.) what is life anyway?

THURSDAY, APRIL 25, 1935: Dad angrily told me Jon was not to see me so much at school—that I could walk to some classes by myself. Somebody (he wouldn't say who) told him we were together too much for our own good. Jon said if he found out who, he would beat him up if it took a club.

The year I became a senior, Jon went to Oklahoma Baptist University. Now I walked alone down the halls; Jon came home often, and we dated enough to keep the appearance of being interested only in each other. I wished other boys would ask me for dates when Jon was away, but, except to play tennis or work on programs, they did not. When Jon came home, I wanted nothing more than to be with him.

SUNDAY, SEPTEMBER 22: At church, I heard Jon's father say Jon would be home next Sunday. I hope so. Mr. Peterson gave me some advice—the same advice everybody gives—only he was awfully nice about it.

WEDNESDAY, OCTOBER 9: Went to prayer meeting with Mom, and it was really good. But at school I am still a wallflower. Went out to the reservoir by myself and cried.

FRIDAY, OCTOBER 11: Jon is here. He came to the football game as soon as he got here and took me home. Oh joy!

SUNDAY, OCTOBER 13: Jon has gone again. It was swell seeing him. He sent me a corsage and spent the afternoon with me. Somehow, it wasn't so hard to let him go this time—I wonder why? Was it because I don't like him as much, or is it because the day was so perfect I could stand it better after the grand afternoon with him? Edris' wedding was this morning; Mrs. Huber sang "Ah, Sweet Mystery of Life." Will I ever find it??

The May I became eighteen, I graduated from Altus High. Daddy stood on the platform handing out diplomas. It was a proud moment for me to have him there and to see his signature on all of my classmates' diplomas. As I passed by, instead of shaking hands, I impulsively gave him a kiss. I was embarrassed at once, but Daddy did not seem to mind.

Now it was time for college, but no decision had been made as to where it would be. There was not much reason to hurry at deciding. During the depression, there was plenty of room in most places of higher learning.

I wanted to go away—a long ways away. I was ready for adventure. I had already been to Tennessee alone, and that was not too far. It was fun to meet new people and do new things!

I think Daddy understood more than anyone else that I wanted to go away. He felt the same way when he was young, and I was like him. But an education was an education. It would not hurt me a bit to go to a state school. The cost would be lower, and he had to pay taxes. Daddy also mentioned O.B.U. After all, he usually said "I'll give twenty-five" every time Dr.

Abernathy led with "I'll give a hundred," whenever the church took an offering for the school. But O.B.U. was at Shawnee, we had relatives there, and I had been there nearly all my life!

Mother had a reason of her own for my not going there: Jon. No, not Jon, really, but the probability of Jon's and my wanting to get married before we completed our educations, if we were on a college campus together. Mother was all for a girls' school for two years. Then she wanted me to go to Baylor. A Baptist school in Texas! Mother sighed with delight every time she thought of it.

I had my own problems about a girls' school: The Altus girls who went to schools we were considering danced. I was tired of being in the group that was never asked to the best parties. I was sure my parents would be as unwilling to allow me to dance at college as they were at home. I would either have to go against their wishes or continue being isolated socially. I had not minded much until now, but I longed to be "in" at college.

Then along came Eleanor. Eleanor's father was holding a city-wide revival in Altus. Our church was co-operating in the meeting, and all the Moores were going every night.

One evening, the evangelist announced that his daughter, who had just graduated from Wheaton College, was coming to spend a few days in Altus to participate in the revival. My mother was the one who offered her a place to stay. She offered her my room, in fact! I had visions of a "preacher's kid," complete with horn-rimmed glasses, hair pulled back in a knot at the back of her head, a big Bible, and sanctimonious phrases.

What came to my room first was a trunk, and it was filled with pretty clothes. Eleanor turned out to be a slender, dimpled girl with short-cut, naturally curly hair. She wore anklets and saddle shoes. She had a Bible all right, and she put it in the middle of the dresser and read it as often as she read letters from her fiancé. And with as much pleasure, to my amazement.

The first night she was at the revival her father asked her to give a testimony. I blushed with embarrassment for her. How *could* he? The only testimony I knew much about was what we had occasionally at prayer meeting. The same few people would say the same few words; then one dear old brother always began testifying. He started in a sing-song voice and went on and on and on and on and on. When he finally sat down, there was no more time for anything. Poor Eleanor.

Eleanor rose with a sunny smile. In words that would do credit to one of Mrs. Peterson's best speech students, she told in a charming, feminine way what the Lord Jesus Christ meant to her. She finished her testimony by going to the piano and playing an arrangement of "There's a Wideness in God's Mercy." Nobody ever before had played the piano like that in Altus. It was ringing, clear music with the touch of authority.

Suddenly, I had an ideal. I wanted to be like Eleanor. My parents also were impressed. At our house, Eleanor was courteous and considerate; her table manners were impeccable. We plied her with questions about Wheaton.

Eleanor showed me her annual. There was no beauty section. "Character is more important at Wheaton," Eleanor said, and showed me pictures of outstanding students in various activities. Eleanor had majored in music. Wheaton had a conservatory of music with the highest rating. And nobody danced.

"Even off the campus?" I asked.

"Not anywhere," said Eleanor.

I was ready to go to Wheaton right that minute. Daddy said the way things worked out made him believe I was intended to go there. Eleanor said she would write for an application. But she made one mistake in front of my doting Mother. She said, "But there are so many who apply, I can't say for sure she'll be accepted."

My Southern Baptist Mother gave us both an unsmiling, level look. "In that case, we will doubtless be able to find some other good school," she said.

MONDAY, JULY 27, 1936: Got a letter from Wheaton accepting me. Jon came to see the letter.

TUESDAY, JULY 28: Went bicycle riding with Jon to the park,

and in the moonlight he asked me to wear his frat pin. I said to wait, and I know it sort of hurt him; but I just can't somehow until I know for sure.

SATURDAY, SEPTEMBER 5: Mother and I have been sewing all day. I have nice clothes for college.

TUESDAY, SEPTEMBER 8: Kitty Boots, a new little kitten, is playing in my trunks, which are ready to be filled with clothes and other things. I leave for Wheaton Saturday.

FRIDAY, SEPTEMBER 11: The last night, and I ache all over. Jon and I went to the football game—but we both felt sad. We didn't say good-by; we both cried and he left. I love him—some way.

SATURDAY, SEPTEMBER 12: On the train and it's air-cooled and I'm about to freeze. Jon sent me a corsage but didn't come to the train. All the family and I cried when the train left.

My tears spilled down on the box that held the lunch Mother had fixed early in the morning. They came unbidden and freely, as though they were commanded by my heart to express something my mind could not fathom. As I looked out the train window and saw Mother and Daddy and David and Virginia standing there, something of joy and sadness made me weep.

It was good-by to being a part of the family as I had been for eighteen years. I was stretching my wings and flying alone, and I felt, rather than understood, at how great a price my wings were given me by the tender, loving care of my parents.

What a far cry it was from the day Daddy left his Tennessee mountains to come to Texas and sleep under the banana trees! He sent me out with blank checks in my purse. Whatever amount was needed to meet my needs would be taken care of by the sweat of his brow, carefully stored up for such a time as this. To him and Mother, it was a dream come true. What they had not been given, they would give.

In time, I wiped my tears away and eagerly watched for what lay ahead. I felt so joyous at going to Wheaton. It was exciting to have it so far away. I knew no one there and no one knew me. I tried to imagine a school where Scripture verses were a part of printing the news, where people talked of the Lord's blessings as naturally as they spoke of lovely sunsets, where ability and character meant more than beauty, and where everyone lived by the same rules!

I signed a statement saying that while I was a student at Wheaton, I would refrain from dancing, drinking, smoking, playing cards, secret societies, and movies. I most cheerfully signed it. Movies were a very small thing to give up in return for a set of rules that would be the same for everyone else as for me.

At Oklahoma City, I changed from the "Doodlebug" to the cool train mentioned in the diary. I spent the night curled up on a double seat in the chair car. Daddy knew I was young and healthy. He would not waste money on unnecessary luxuries.

The next morning, I stepped off the train into the smoky station at St. Louis. It was hot, as hot as Oklahoma, and I had expected the weather to become cooler as we went farther north. I ignored the waiting redcaps and carried my suitcase up the long corridor to the station and back to the next train. My arm ached by the time I put the suitcase down, but I was not going to waste money on unnecessary luxuries, either.

The train to Chicago was the first streamliner I ever saw. It was glistening and sleek, and it had a name all its own—The Abraham Lincoln. When I walked into the spacious chair car, I felt I was indeed in a new world.

Chicago's Union Station filled me with wonder. How late everyone seemed to be to wherever they were going! They strode along with unsmiling faces as though they had already missed a connection.

I knew Wheaton was a suburb of Chicago, and I still had a piece of my ticket to take me there. But everyone seemed to take for granted I knew how to make the rest of the trip. The ticket called for a change to another station.

"But it would be easier to take the 'el,'" the conductor of the streamliner told me. "They'll tell you where to catch it at the station."

At the station I asked not once but several times before I finally found my way to the el platform. It was high above the street, and then I remembered about Chicago's elevated trains from our trip to the world's fair.

I showed the conductor my ticket as I got on. "You can't use that on here, lady," he said bitterly.

"But they told me I could—or I thought that was what they meant," I floundered.

"Lady, you have to have an el ticket to ride the elevated." I could tell he was not interested in explaining anything to me, but I balked at buying a ticket when I already had one. ("Blood will tell," Daddy said.)

I went back to the Union Station, got Parmelee service to the Great Northern Railroad, and went to Wheaton as directed by the ticket Daddy had bought me.

I have often thought of standing there on the el platform that sunny September afternoon in Chicago. It was strangely deserted at the moment. I can remember the pigeons flying down to pick up bits of popcorn or peanuts they found there. I am sure Mother was praying for me, and Daddy was working harder than ever before.

In the pictures in Eleanor's annual, Wheaton had seemed a very beautiful place. To me it was a clean page, a time of beginning, a turn in the path no eye could see save God alone. I could hardly wait to make the turn.

7

At Last

I've Found You

Wheaton was even more beautiful than the pictures in the annual. The campus walks were lined with giant elms and willows. Even from third- and fourth-story windows I had to look up to see the tops of the soft sugar maples, whose leaves were beginning to turn as red as an Oklahoma sunset. Among them, beautiful, old, ivy-covered Blanchard Hall rose like a turreted, white-stone fortress.

Close by, in the same architectural style, was a girls' dormitory built of red brick and known as the Red Castle. I did not stay there. I was one of the fortunate freshman girls who was to have a room in the almost completed New Dorm across the street to the north. Until it was finished, we were temporarily housed in local homes.

I relished the walk from the Olander house to Bartlett Dining Hall and the campus. The maples had turned red, an unbelievable red, and the elms were an unbelievable golden yellow. Perhaps I was so impressed because this was the first September since I was in the second grade that I had been anywhere except on the parched, brown school grounds of my native state. No wonder Daddy yearned for his Tennnessee trees! Wheaton's grass was green and moist. The emerald sweep of it down the length of the front campus was utterly beautiful to me.

I came to love the little suburb. There was a lake which froze over in the winter for skating, and I had never ice skated before. I found crocuses and valley lilies in the early spring around the old First Baptist Church, and I never saw a more exquisite rose window than the little one over the nave of Gary Memorial Methodist Church.

"Town" was, for the most part, a row of stores facing the maze of railroad tracks leading into Chicago. For awhile, I kept hearing the clanging bells as the safety gates went down and the noisy trains rushed by, but soon I did not notice them at all.

Wheaton had soot and I did not like that. But people seemed to have the same attitude toward it as we had for dust, so I tried to act accordingly. Who minded a little soot when the grass was emerald green and the trees grew tall with red and gold leaves?

Close to Blanchard Hall, with walks leading to it from all directions, was the building we called "the Stupe." It was the post office, the soda fountain, the book store, and somewhere behind that, the gymnasium. On its steps, freshmen sang songs at sophomores' requests. There people met and walked to the conservatory of music auditorium for chapel.

On either side of the main walk to the Stupe from Blanchard Hall were flowers and shrubs and the towering trees. It was there my roommate, Ruth, and I were walking one of my first mornings at Wheaton. The sky was blue and it was so warm I wore a summer dress. The dress was yellow and had round gold buttons and very short sleeves. It was an extra nice one Mother got on sale at Russell's department store.

Ruth called to someone and said, "I want you to meet . . ."

I did not pay much attention to what she was saying. There was so much to see, so many interesting things going on.

"Connie, this is Boyd Hunt from Creston, Iowa. Boyd, this is my roommate from Oklahoma . . . "

I wonder now, I really wonder, that a scarlet tanager did not fly through the trees, or a cardinal break into his high, clear call, or why some sound of stringed instruments and organs did not crescendo into a great symphony of music. How could I have looked into those deep, merry, blue eyes and not recognize what I had been looking for all my life?

"Hi there!" I said.

"Hello, Connie," said Boyd.

He and Ruth exchanged pleasant words about last summer in Indianapolis where Boyd sold Bibles. I hardly listened. My diary records not a word about the event. I do remember noticing how he said my name. Boyd said it with a soft *o*. "Connie." I liked it, but I supposed it was a Yankee way of talking.

Evidently, I made a great impression on him. It was May before he even walked across the campus with me.

September at Wheaton began for me a wonderful time of fun and thrills, heartaches and laughter, filled in, pressed down, and running over. When everyone lived by the same rules, there seemed to me to be pure freedom. Except for a single heart-tugging memory back home, it was a little touch of heaven on earth.

Wheaton was a place of music. Everything began with singing. And such singing! There were more fellows than girls enrolled in the college, and a richness of tenor and bass filled every song. In high school, it was a job to get the boys to sing even at pep rallies. To hear the student body at Wheaton sing the alma mater was a spine-tingling experience. When they sang "Wonderful Grace of Jesus," I dropped out after the first two lines. Some emotion in my heart put a lump in my throat and drew tears from my eyes. No one was urging people to sing. They just sang. Over a thousand tongues were singing their great Redeemer's praise. It was a week before I could control my tears of joy and sing aloud as well as from my bursting heart.

Wheaton abounded in kindness. Each freshman girl had a "Big Sister" in the junior class. Bewilderment was met with understanding explanation. There were no sororities or fraternities. The literary societies were the hub of social activities, and their aim was to be as inclusive, not exclusive, as possible. Every student had a standing invitation to join any society, and it was the society which considered itself honored.

To be wanted, to be understood—what a happy year that

meant for any freshman! There were, no doubt, other things that helped me. Mother's sewing, for instance. An aunt of mine told me to wear every outfit I had the first week. I tried.

There were over four hundred of us in the new class of '40, and we were then the largest class ever to have entered Wheaton. The question over whether to raise enrolment quotas was argued from then on. That too was the year they decided to raise the scholastic standards, which, I feel sure, was the reason for my grades in botany.

Or maybe the trouble with botany was lab. It was my first experience with a laboratory science, and I kept seeing things under the microscope which had no relation to the project we were studying. They were so interesting that I asked Bill—the tall, red-haired, senior football player who was lab assistant—to come see what I found.

Bill would amble over, view my find, look at me with mingled disgust and amazement, and say laconically, "Something of cosmic significance, no doubt."

I drew what I saw, labeled it "Something of Cosmic Significance," and everyone at our table thought it was pretty funny. Only I did not feel so happy when the grades came out.

When it came to grades, Wheaton was as hard as nails. Every semester there was weeping and gnashing of teeth. Even my piano teacher, Mr. Van Dusen, the kindest of men, turned to steel when it came to giving high grades. When I saw my grade in piano the first semester, I came to Mr. Van Dusen in tears. My woe moved him not at all.

"Crying will not help you, Connie Betty," he said. "What you need to do is work."

For Mr. Van Dusen, I worked. I learned to listen eagerly to what he said and to remember it when I got to my practice room. Soon I settled into a routine of study and class work, as did the majority of students. Other things were important, but they had to be fitted into the main reason we were at college.

Unfortunately, I did not write home in a way to convey what the main thing was at college. I wrote home much like I wrote in my diary. What news would it be to say, "I studied three hours on French today"? Nor did I realize some of the deep, lasting things happening to me. My roommate, for instance. My diary rarely mentions her name, and I did not write my parents much about her because our friendship was a slow and steady growth like a tree planted by the waters.

Neither Ruth Schnicke nor I had ever shared a room with anyone before. Ruth's father was a businessman like mine. Some very wise person in the dean's office no doubt took our backgrounds into account. Ruth's family was Baptist. Both of us were brought up with the same ideas, and Roomie often said, "Connie and I always get all we want; we just know what to want."

I learned to love and appreciate Ruth as I did no other girl. She was steady, unselfish, and sincere. My parents wanted me to have a friend like that, and they would have delighted in a letter on the subject, as well as on my study of French or botany. But what did I write home about? Why, the fellows, of course! The dates and the parties and concerts and flowers I got made the real news of the day.

One day that first week, I wore the red, velveteen skirt and jacket Mother made. ("That skirt isn't as big as a minute," a neighbor had said.) I strongly advise every freshman girl to have her mother make her a red, velveteen skirt and jacket. As I walked down the steps from the Stupe, some sophomore fellows called "Button, Frosh!" I reached up to touch the button on the top of the bright-green cap marking me as a freshman. It was a lovely day, a simply lovely day.

THURSDAY, SEPTEMBER 17: I'm all registered, I passed all the tests, and got to take eighteen hours. I wrote checks to pay for everything and I'm ready to work.

FRIDAY, SEPTEMBER 18: Just back from faculty reception. Met all classes half-time today and like them. Took physical exam and tried out for glee club. Got a swell letter from Jon and two pieces of cake from Mom. Sang for sophs on gym steps!!

SATURDAY, SEPTEMBER 26: It's raining and I walked bare-headed in it and pretended Jon was with me because we've had, oh, so much fun in the rain. I miss the folks tonight, too.

SUNDAY, SEPTEMBER 27: September is slipping by with me wondering whether I am silly or really in love with Jon, and if so, why I should stay here and ache and ache for him. Wheaton is wonderful, but I want Jon. Some boys are rushing me.

SUNDAY, OCTOBER 5: Had dates with Robert (walking to park) and Venson (church) and Robert asked me for two more (which I refused—already had them). And after supper at Bartlett, two nice boys (from Florida and Georgia) walked home with me.

FRIDAY, OCTOBER 9: After the Phil informal, had a date with Iner and he was very nice—kind of bashful so I liked him. Got a typewriter, blanket, and dress from home today. Swell letter from Jon, and I miss him so much.

SATURDAY, OCTOBER 10: Football game with Roger (freshman, New York City) and date tonight with Dave (junior, Chicago). They were so nice.

TUESDAY, OCTOBER 13: Robert came into my practice room and walked to Bartlett with me and ate with me and then walked home with me—*and* said sweet things.

SATURDAY, OCTOBER 31: Tower Concert with Robert. He was *very* nice tonight and somehow—I don't know why—I told him about "Cherry-Ripe" when he wanted to kiss me good night. Why did I tell him that? Do I care what he thinks? I wonder what the Lord brought me here for? I do think he did. I wonder if I really love Jon? I miss him so—and, yes, love him—somehow. I don't understand. "I think you're wonderful. Good night, plenty-sweet."—Robert.

WEDNESDAY, NOVEMBER 18: Andy walked to Bartlett with me. Robert followed and ate with me and walked me home. Andy said Bob wanted a date to the men's glee club party with me but found out Paul had it. I refused Warren and don't like Paul more than others, but he asked first. Now Iner just called for the same date—oh dear, I like him and had to refuse.

FRIDAY, DECEMBER 4: It's 12:30 and I'm packing to move into the new Dorm! It's so exciting and the dorm is perfect. Had a date after lit with Andy and he was swell. He's from Baltimore.

SATURDAY, DECEMBER 5: We're in the New Dorm, and it's simply perfect. It's raining tonight, too, and Andy carried me from the taxi to where it was dry. It was after his open house. He was swell and he's nice to me and we had such fun. I like Andy. *I like everybody!*

FRIDAY, FEBRUARY 19, 1937: The Washington banquet with Andy, and he sent me a white orchid! I'm so thrilled over everything. I was on the program, and Andy and I took pictures afterward. "You're sweet, you're beautiful. Thanks, Connie."—Andy

Jon wrote in March that he was chosen as final speaker for his college revival. I was so proud and happy.

WEDNESDAY, MARCH 3: Got a swell letter from Dad with a check in it which I can really use. It was like spring today.

FRIDAY, APRIL 30: This afternoon I practiced with Robert for a program, and he asked me if I still had never been kissed on the lips, and of course I hadn't. He told me he had bet money on me that I hadn't. When I thought of how he thought of me, I came home and prayed. I believe the Lord heard my prayers, but never in all my life have I felt this way.

Why don't I fall in love? I can't see one step ahead. It's just blank. And so I'm trusting him to guide me step by step. I will follow with his strength.

Tonight Andy and I weren't saying anything, and finally I asked what the matter was. He told me he was never going to say he loved me again until he could say what he wanted to afterward. Then he acted unhappy and I can't see why he needs to say anything afterward and I wish he'd quit *acting so awful.*

SATURDAY, MAY 8: A perfect day in May. Began at 6:30 A.M. playing tennis with Jim and went bicycle riding with him this afternoon and had a soda in the Stupe afterward. Also in the afternoon took a walk with Andy. It was warm and I wore my blue and white dress. Andy picked apple blossoms and put them in my hair.

TUESDAY, MAY 11: Just got back from oratorical contest. Jim got third place and he was simply swell! I was floored—I had no idea he was so good at it! His voice is very rich and deep.

I began praying for Jim that June and asking the Lord to show me what to do. Jim had asked for a date to go scooter riding, so we did. And coming home I asked him if he knew the Lord. When he said he did not, I told him the best I could how wonderful the Lord was. Before he left, he said he really wanted to find him and he would try before he went to sleep.

MONDAY, JUNE 7: Jimmie and I walked awhile today, and he does know the Lord. I'm so glad! He has his own ideas about things—especially hell (he doesn't believe in it), but he even seems different today. He's really nice too. "You should never belong to just one man. You were born to be the darling of soldiers in the camp."—Jimmie. The way he said it in his deep, beautiful voice made shivers run up my back, only—well, I would like to be like Florence Nightingale. But also I would like just one man, somewhere, to belong to.

Toward the end of my freshman year, Daddy could stand it no longer. "You are not getting out of college what I sent you there for," he wrote, "and you will not go back to Wheaton."

This news threw me into such a thrum I forgot a piano lesson and spread the horrible news among the girls in New Dorm, who promptly had a prayer meeting for me. I wrote wildly home for an explanation of what I had done, and Mother answered that Daddy had the notion I was spending all my time and thoughts on the young men of the campus instead of my studies. I replied in a pleading letter to Daddy to consider my grades, which *had* improved, as an indication I was really learning something and spending time to do it, and to please, please not decide I could not return to Wheaton.

Daddy immediately wrote that if I felt so strongly about the college I could be assured of returning. I was sure Mother said all the right things, the girls rejoiced with me, Mr. Van Dusen arranged a time to make up my lesson, and I was more careful what I wrote home.

I quickly discovered one thing not to write home about at all. A girl came to visit at Olander house one day, and I liked her a lot. She told us how she was working for her room and board at a home where she lived in an attic room infested by rats. I was horrified at her story and wrote Daddy all about it. I was sure he would send money for her in the next mail.

Daddy wrote me a scorching letter saying he was working night and day to send his own children to college and for me to spend my time studying for an education instead of talking to the girls all night.

You can imagine my amazement when I read a letter to him that began, "Dear Mr. Moore: I want to thank you for the check you sent. I am so grateful to you because I would not be in college this semester except for your help . . . ." Mother showed it to me one day when we were looking at things she kept in her cedar chest.

Daddy visited Wheaton during my sophomore year. He came by on his way to Washington to attend the Small Business Men's convention. Being on the campus was the magic that put him on Wheaton's band wagon, and he gladly paid the bills, not only for me, but also for my sister who attended Wheaton later. What impressed him most were the fellows working in the kitchens. Daddy considered work something to be thankful for, and these boys were laughing and singing as they worked. "Singing what sounded like religious songs," said he approvingly.

Daddy evidently could live without hearing about the fellows in every letter, but I think Mother rather enjoyed it. She remembered the days I walked the halls alone, and she was glad for how it was now.

WEDNESDAY, MAY 5: The fellow, Boyd Hunt, who talked to me at Williston open house walked across the campus with me today. He asked for a date to open lit.

SATURDAY, MAY 8: Refused Andy a date to open lit, which I may regret—Boyd may forget. He hasn't said a word about what time to come for me or anything.

FRIDAY, MAY 14: What a day! Boyd didn't call to ask what time to come so I started with the other girls without dates and met him coming in the door. We both stopped and he said, "Well, this is service!" The girls went on and left us standing there. He said he thought I'd know he'd come in time to get us to open lit. He was so sorry and so swell about it that I went back upstairs and changed to my formal, and we went and had fun. He bought me a box of candy and said it was the most enjoyable evening he ever had.

SATURDAY, MAY 15: Everyone is impressed about my date with Boyd. I hadn't told anyone who my date to open lit was, so they didn't know until they saw him. Jane says, "The very way he carries himself spells character." Good night! He must be awfully conceited and I never intend to date him again if he asks me, which he hasn't.

SUNDAY, MAY 23: Spent the afternoon walking to Glen Ellyn and back (after strawberry malts) with Boyd, who came to ask for another date. All the girls think he's wonderful, and I think he's just nice. They said he's been elected president of the junior class for next year, but what's that compared to preaching at the college revival like Jon or national champion debaters, etc.?

TUESDAY, MAY 25: Today I got a special delivery air mail letter from Jon, and tonight he called me to say happy birthday.

WEDNESDAY, MAY 26: My nineteenth birthday, and such fun! Lunch at Bartlett with Robert, swell letters and a cake and card from home, and tonight dinner with Andy. He had, with Roomie, fixed a surprise—candles, cake and all—and everybody sang happy birthday. Andy also sent me flowers. Tonight the girls came in to eat Mom's cake. Roomie got ice cream, and the cake went around just right. Stanton sent a gift and letter, and loads of people were nice to me. Thank you, dear Lord.

THURSDAY, MAY 27: Dinner at Betty's and afterwards *Smilin' Thru'* (Senior expression recital) with Boyd and another boy and a girl Boyd has dated and likes—the idea of which I didn't like too much. I had the feeling he was comparing me with her, but he was nice, and I felt a thousand different ways. Why does *Smilin' Thru'* come into my life again? It's my favorite story and favorite song.

On Saturday I went to the Friar's party on Fox River with Boyd. We canoed for hours and talked about everything—even the mission field. He was willing to go anywhere, too. I said if I ever went to Africa I would grow orchids in the yard. He said I was the only girl he had ever met who could think—but I did not know what he meant by that.

He had brought games and books (O. Henry) along in the canoe for fear he would be bored. I almost didn't go with him when I realized he was so afraid of running out of conversation in three hours. He even admitted it, but ended up saying it was the best time he ever had. He made me so exasperated, and yet I liked for him to be so honest.

MONDAY, JUNE 7: Played tennis with Roomie and had two finals today. Got a letter from Daddy saying he was wiring my ticket home and for me to pick it up in Chicago Union Station.

SATURDAY, JUNE 12: The Lord was kind and sent me Boyd today. He was swell. He tied my trunks and helped me get tickets for them. We drank cold Cokes up in my room when we finished everything.

SUNDAY, JUNE 13: Boyd was on the gospel team with me tonight. He was nice. He's going into Chi with me to the train.

MONDAY, JUNE 14: Boyd and I left Wheaton pretty early (I ate breakfast with the girls, and cried when I saw the Tower thru' the trees for the last time) (and the girls sang "God be with you till we meet again" out the windows as I left) but when we got to Chicago there was no ticket.

Boyd left to go back to his work at the dining hall; and also he had promised to help Emily get *her* trunks to the train. So I wired Daddy, and he wired money for the ticket. I got it, but I couldn't make the train—well, I guess I could have if I had run. But my suitcase was too heavy to try that, so I waited for a later train.

Boyd called the station, because even though he said he would try to get back, he knew he couldn't make it in time if I caught the first train. But the operator said that I had left. He came back anyhow and found me and called me precious, and held my hand tight in both of his, and said it was the happiest hour of his life. Gee! Just when I needed someone. Boyd is the most different boy I have ever met.

TUESDAY, JUNE 15: Home again and am I tired and sleepy! Everyone is teasing Daddy about forgetting to have my ticket in Chicago on time. I really didn't mind because it worked out all right. The folks met me at the train. Bobbie called. Jon came down and I feel like a hypocrite.

WEDNESDAY, JUNE 16: Talked to the folks and the kids most all day and it was swell. My big trunk came, and Daddy looked at it and asked, "Who tied your trunk?" I said, "A boy at school—Boyd Hunt." He said, "That trunk is really tied right." Daddy is impressed by the strangest things. Went to prayer meeting with Jon tonight, but it isn't the same somehow. Nothing is wrong with him—it's just me who is all at sea about myself.

SATURDAY, JUNE 26: Worked at the grainhouse most all day. Life is very strange. If I could only be sure of myself—but I'm not, so I don't know what to do. Jon? Wheaton? Love?

WEDNESDAY, JUNE 30: June has flitted past, and tonight I feel like the biggest flop in the world. I lost my temper; looked daggers at Jon during prayer meeting (I don't know why). And worst of all, I can't remember having my devotions this morning.

TUESDAY, JULY 6: Jon took me to the mountains, and we watched the sunset. It was too good to talk about.

WEDNESDAY, JULY 7: Jon took me to prayer meeting and afterward we played monopoly. "You're mean—sweetness—I love you. If you were normal we'd have been married long ago."—Jon

SUNDAY, JULY 11: Jon came in the afternoon, and tonight I felt so secure and contented with him while we rode around.

SATURDAY, JULY 24: Got a swell letter from Boyd. This morning on the tennis court someone called me, and it sounded the way he says my name. I'm lonesome for Wheaton.

SUNDAY, JULY 25: Jon preached at our church, and it was simply wonderful. Mother invited him to dinner afterward.

THURSDAY, JULY 29: Another swell evening with Jon. Gee! He almost convinced me we could live happily ever after. He has written his college about me and got a letter saying I could get a scholarship. If I were sure . . .

FRIDAY, AUGUST 6: "I love you with all my heart. Will you marry me?"—Jon. "Yes."—Connie. We were watching for shooting stars out in the front yard. He kissed me on the lips and we prayed. He's going to talk to Daddy tomorrow, and that scares me to death. What will he say? I am upstairs in my room trying to decide whether or not to tell Mother, when I go down to the sleeping porch. When I opened my Bible just now, it was at 2 Kings 7:9: "We do not well: this day is a day of good tidings, and we hold our peace: if we tarry till the morning light, some mischief will come upon us: now therefore come, that we may go and tell the King's household." My engagement should be good tidings, so I will tell mother. But I'm sort of scared or something.

SATURDAY, AUGUST 7: Mother was sweet and didn't seem at all surprised. She hugged me and said it was late and we'd better talk about it in the morning. But I slept hardly at all last night, and at seven this morning I called Jon and told him it was no use—I just couldn't—and I cried, and he was absolutely swell and I don't deserve it. "Sweetheart, don't cry. It's all right. I love you"—Jon.

The *Altus Times Democrat* said stars fell on Oklahoma that night, so I feel sure they did, but I did not see them. Becoming engaged and being really kissed for the first time was not what I expected it to be. And never in any thought of my whole life had I dreamed that so momentous a decision would be rescinded in less than twelve hours.

Perhaps you are disillusioned as you read this. If you are very young, or a fairy story perfectionist as I was, I am sure you are. But this is not a fairy tale, and it falls far short of perfection. I wanted the cherries to be ripe, but that did not make them so. Maybe if I had not found the verse in the Bible, if I had not told Mother, if—but you see how it was.

You see how Jon was, too. And now you wait, because his story is not finished either. The trouble with Jon and me was that we thought time was running out, when it was just beginning.

That was the exception to "Cherry-Ripe," but I did not toss the ideal away. I made a mistake, and I despised my bewildering behavior. But the whole truth was that the sweet mystery of life was not yet solved, and there was still a hope in my heart it someday would be.

Jon and I tried to go on as though nothing had happened. We had known each other for a long time, and our friendship was no shallow thing. Jon's preaching appointments took him out of town more often than not, and I spent a lot of time working in the Intermediate Sunday school department.

Mr. Peterson asked me to substitute for him, while he and Mrs. Peterson were away during the summer, as superintendent of the Intermediate department. I was amazed that he thought I could do even a substitute job, but the challenge of such an opportunity set my mind whirling with ideas. I had seen and heard the gospel presented in scintillating ways at school. Now I could try to help the Intermediates as I had been helped. I planned ahead. I used object lessons. I prayed. I asked the teachers to pray with me for the unsaved young people in the department. Several of the teachers and I came early on Sunday morning for a preservice prayer meeting.

I came home from my first year at college not feeling intellectually superior to anyone; but theologically I considered myself an authority. I had learned the difference between a modernist and a fundamentalist. (You *had* to be one or the other.) It was easy to tell. A modernist mostly talked about how God was love, and a fundamentalist always mentioned the blood of Christ cleansing us from all sin. In Wheaton chapel, we decided in which category a speaker fell after a few sentences.

Modernists in chapel were as scarce as hen's teeth, but we heard a lot about them. Mostly we heard about them from the sophomores and juniors, who knew much about such things. Sometimes the chapel speakers told about modernistic churches or even missionaries. I heard it said that some large Southern denominations had more "churchianity" than Christianity, but since no names were mentioned, I let it pass.

I had a belligerent attitude, however, when missionaries were labled modernistic. I intended to speak my piece to anyone who said anything against Southern Baptist missionaries, but no one ever did. Instead, I heard them called by name and praised as good soldiers of the faith. This was as it should be, I thought. Perhaps we Southern Baptists could stand a little criticism, but our missionaries were a different matter.

There were more Baptist students at Wheaton than those from any other denomination, but within the suburb was only one Baptist church, a Northern Baptist church. Roomie and I went to visit there, but it did not seem Baptist to me at all. There were very few young people; there was no Training Union as I knew it, and the music sounded like old, old recordings. I think it was the music more than anything else that pushed me away.

But to be more fair, I should admit it might have been something I did not realize at the time. All my life I had belonged to the biggest and most popular church in town. In Wheaton, the churches most attended by students were three. One was housed in a new building. It looked clean to the point of being sterile. Inside, I was sure there was a time to smile, but I was apprehensive of smiling at the wrong time. When the services were over, I wondered if the Bible, especially parts of it, had been worshiped more than Christ.

The most popular church was Congregational and was called College Church of Christ. I really do not know how I passed it by except that its name sounded too Campbellite to a Southerner.

The church I chose met in a lodge building and was called

the Tabernacle, or just Tab by the students who made up the
majority of the membership. The pastor was an upperclassman at
the college. His sermons were a blessing to me, and I found
myself constantly praying for him as he stood there preaching.
The back pages of the Bible I used that year are full of quotes
from Johnny's sermons.

Even more of an impression was made on me by the group
of Swedish Christians who formed the nucleus of the church.
To this day I have never known a group of people who more
personified "faith, virtue, knowledge, temperance, patience, god-
liness, brotherly kindness, love." In order to join the church, I
was asked to go to a small room in the rear of the auditorium.
There prospective members met with several of the older members of the church. An elderly, white-haired, Swedish gentleman
asked me to tell him of my experience in becoming a Christian.
I tried to explain what Christ meant to me. He listened, nodding
his head, and in Swedish accent said softly, "Praise the Lord."
When I finished, he welcomed me as a member of the church.

All this I related in letters home to Mother and Daddy. Their
return mail on the subject was casual. Several years later I found
they had talked to the pastor. He suggested that since no letter
of membership had been requested, the whole matter could be
treated as a watchcare provision. It was a long time before it
occurred to me that I might have been dismissed from my home
church for heresy!

It was traditional among Wheaton students that only engaged
couples had church dates on Sunday mornings. So Sunday school
was really a school, and I reveled in what seemed real Bible
study. Where a quarterly had heretofore been my main textbook,
with perhaps a few verses of Scripture read at the beginning of
the lesson, now the Bible was all. What a joy it was to have an
open Bible and a red pencil and someone to make the verses
come alive. Usually the teacher was a professor from the college.
I do not remember whether we studied a series of related subjects, or one book of the Bible, or if we mostly had devotional
lessons from different texts. I do know that from that Sunday

school study, parts of the Scriptures became good food to me. I cherish the blessing of them yet.

The evening service was a time for dating and had more social flavor. After church there was usually a young people's sing and testimony service with refreshments. It soon became a rare experience for me to attend the evening services, however, because I began to go out in the Chicago area with the gospel teams.

A group of young people with an adult supervisor would leave the campus late Sunday afternoon to go to places not too far away which were like a different world: the Pacific Garden mission, small dark churches, and street meetings.

I remember one rescue mission where I played the piano. Somewhere beyond us, a meal was being prepared for the men. Somewhere near, was there a laundry? The odors blended together with those from the poorly clad men in the audience. I was ashamed that I felt almost ill. These were people for whom Christ died, and I found it hard to endure a short time in their presence. But I did not mind with my heart—it was my stomach that was so carnal. We were invited to stay for supper after the service. Fortunately for me, the leader declined because of the necessity of reaching the campus on schedule.

On the way back, with the clean fresh air blowing through the car window, I wondered what had been accomplished in that service by our gospel team. I had no doubt that God's Word would not return unto him void, but had those men heard it—those sleepy, bleary-eyed, impoverished men? And had I contributed anything toward helping those men find God? As I played the piano, I searched my mind for a melody that would mean something to them. Certainly not the choruses that were so refreshing to me. These men seemed old. I remembered songs Daddy tried to sing to us— "songs we sang in the little church when I was a little boy." Would these men have heard "Tell Mother I'll Be There"? I could not be sure. "There is a Fountain"? I finally decided on "The Old Rugged Cross" for my special number. Surely they had heard it sung, and perhaps some memory would help them listen to the sermon to follow.

Another gospel team on another Sunday went to a small church in the area. We understood the church was becoming modernistic. We were asked to come help interest the young people in the things of the Lord. I did not question the logic of a "modernistic church" asking a "fundamentalist young people's group" to help them do anything. I do not remember that evening with delight. It was evident we were invited over the protest of many at the insistence of a few. The few were cordial to the point of overstatement; and the many, including the pastor who made only a brief appearance, merely acknowledged our presence with an unsmiling nod. *We don't belong here,* I thought. Nothing went too well that evening.

I especially remember a street meeting one night on Chicago's South side. There was no piano playing that night, and I went only to help with the singing. Several adults were along, and while we had the street meeting, the girls were in the center of the group while the fellows and adults formed a semicircle around them facing the small platform on the street. One of the fellows spoke, and people, mostly men, stopped a minute to listen.

"I am a college student," said the speaker, "but I came to college without money and without knowing how I could stay in school. God has supplied all my needs in ways I never dreamed possible. He can and will supply your needs, too, through our Lord Jesus . . . ." People only paused to listen and then walked on. We sang and prayed. It was an exhilarating experience. People listened because they chose to listen. When they wanted to, they left. I liked being on a gospel team.

While I was away at school, a new pastor came to our Altus church. It took only one auditing of his sermons for me to decide he was a modernist. Not wanting to be hypocritical, I decided to tell him so. I believe, afterwards, he forgave me. Or else he just considered the source and thought nothing of it. I am not so sure about his wife. "Why do you think I am a modernist?" he asked.

"Because," I answered without the slightest qualm, "You didn't once mention the blood of Christ in your sermon."

"That is true," he replied, "but do you remember I asked people to believe in him as their Saviour?"

I admitted this but pointed out that such terminology was rather vague. How many other things I pointed out, I cannot recall. I do not want to be too hard on myself. Even though I was conceited and off-center, my heart was warm with love for the Lord and I longed to *do something*. And in my young, freshman way, I did something.

I tried to use all the best of what I remembered of the past year. I spent a good part of my time working on new ways to present old truths. The young people listened, and the adult leaders, who for the most part were family friends, sang my praises to Mother and Daddy.

Dear Mother and Daddy! I feel sure they were proud one minute and utterly disgusted the next. Mother without doubt saw straight through me. I did not rise a great while before day to have my devotions, but I spent much time in the mornings reading my Bible and marking it with a red pencil. I was late for breakfast, and Mother finished the dishes by the time I got downstairs to present myself to the rest of the family with the superior air of one who underlined more verses in red pencil than anyone else. My brother and sister were signally unimpressed, and I think the whole family breathed a sigh of relief when I was packed and off to school again.

The world of a sophomore was a new and different one. I loved college more than ever. But at my adopted church things changed ever so slightly. The Sunday school was being taught by another teacher in a different way from the year before. There was much debate, which I am sure was thoroughly enjoyed by many. For the first time I wondered when the church had an election of teachers and officers.

Shortly afterward I was asked to help in a church in the Chicago area during Sunday school and junior church. I gladly accepted, and my Sundays gradually became a series of services in different churches. More often than not, I happened to be on the same gospel team with another Baptist, Boyd Hunt.

MONDAY, SEPTEMBER 13: Wheaton again, and it's glorious to see everyone. Boyd met me at Union Station and got us bananas and cream. I tried to convince him they were better without sugar. Saw Andy and my heart turned a flip. Robert took me to town.

TUESDAY, SEPTEMBER 14: Roomie is here, and she brought me a bracelet from Rome! Boyd took care of my trunks and has been so nice till tonight when we loyal sophomores were teasing the frosh. He said, *to us*: "Booooooo!"

WEDNESDAY, SEPTEMBER 15: I had a date with Boyd, and he said, "I love you." I told him about Jon, but he only said, "I love you." I'm kind of in a daze.

THURSDAY, SEPTEMBER 16: Tomorrow school begins and I'm really going to work hard. Boyd ate breakfast and lunch with me and said, "I love you." I told him he couldn't possibly love me because he didn't know me long enough and not to tease about such serious things.

FRIDAY, SEPTEMBER 17: The faculty reception, and am I tired after taking my little sisters around. Boyd was there.

MONDAY, SEPTEMBER 20: Andy and I went walking this afternoon and he tried to tell me something, he said, but he didn't. I played for services tonight, and it was fun even though I was scared. Afterward Boyd came over and said he was proud of me. Then he walked home with me. He was so swell. "I'm the luckiest boy on the campus tonight, punkin' "—Boyd.

TUESDAY, SEPTEMBER 21: This morning Andy was walking to chapel with me, and Boyd came up and said, "Hi, Andy—hi, Connie." Somehow he was walking between Andy and me, and he and Andy were talking and laughing, and when we got to chapel, *Boyd* walked me to my seat. Later he came to the dorm and talked to me, and he was so swell I threw a kiss out the window to him as he left. I didn't really mean to, but he makes me feel—well—I guess—happy.

WEDNESDAY, SEPTEMBER 22: It is Indian summer and the trees are glorious. This afternoon Boyd and I studied together outside in front of the tower. He got down on the grass to read his book beside where I was sitting. And once when I looked over at him, he was looking at me, and he said, "Even if you're never mine, I'll always thank the Lord for just loving you." No one ever said anything like that to me before, and I never felt this way before.

After that, it was all over but the shoutin', and everyone knew it except me and (I like to hope) Boyd. My other boy friends folded their tents and silently left me alone. I had the feeling they liked Boyd better than me! Even Jon, when Boyd came to Altus in December and sought Jon out for a talk, told me with a queer look, "I always knew you'd meet someone like that." My parents, my brother, and my sister took to him as naturally as breathing. Only Daddy tried to put a time limit on things eventually—and then it was too late.

That year Boyd was a junior at Wheaton. He was working his way through school by washing dishes and serving tables in the dining halls. He was also a cheer leader for the intercollegiate games. His energy was boundless, and he knew everybody on the campus. Someone told me in a "so there" way one day, "He's nicest to you, but he's nice to everyone."

Under the glass of my desk is a clipping from our church paper with a print of one of Boyd's prayers. It ends with: "Bless the unsaved everywhere." Prayers for the unsaved familiar to me often ask the Lord to "convict the unsaved of their sins and bring them to the cross." And I am sure Boyd would be the first to say that was the only way they could be truly blessed. But to me it is a picture of what he is—asking the Lord to bless them.

He never seemed to worry. Especially, he never seemed to worry about me. Other boys, when I did not return their affections, at one time or another became angry and declared they would get them another girl, or said they would leave school, or even threatened to jump in the Chicago River. I never actually believed such threats, but at least I knew they cared.

Nothing I did or said seemed capable of provoking Boyd to either anger or despair. I finally asked him one day, "Don't you ever worry about me—I mean us?"

He looked at me like the age of innocence. "Don't you know the Bible says it's a sin to worry?" he asked. "A Christian is supposed to rejoice evermore. The Lord will take care of the future."

The only time he deviated from such a philosophy was when we quarreled once after we were engaged. That afternoon he told me he might as well join the French Foreign Legion, and walked off and left me standing there. For some inexplicable reason, I believed he would do just that, had hysterics up in my room, and vomited all night long. As bad as Jeanette was about Bob, and you know how bad that was! Oh well, it's too late now.

After Boyd said that no matter what happened, he would still be thankful, I went to my practice room and wrote a song. It does not mention love—I honestly did not think I was in love—but I can see it was there. The words began: "You're so wonderful, you make me feel just like a queen who sits upon a throne . . . ."

FRIDAY, SEPTEMBER 24: In the *Gay Gargoyle* today it said, "And it's Moore fun to go Hunting this season"—and are Boyd and I being teased?! We walked after services tonight.

SATURDAY, SEPTEMBER 25: I mostly wasted time today till tonight when I studied. Rosa and Ruth Bell have been talking Chinese to each other. It's like music to hear them. Their mother and daddy are missionaries in China.

MONDAY, SEPTEMBER 27: This morning I got fifteen roses from Boyd! I was so thrilled and he's so nice. He said, "They aren't half as sweet as you." I'm gradually getting my lessons.

One night just as I had finished some letters, a bunch of boys from Clark's (where Boyd lived) came by singing "When Irish Eyes Are Smiling." Then they all yelled, "Hello, Connie!!!" I nearly died! The girls really teased me! But I just loved it.

FRIDAY, OCTOBER 8: The informal is over and it was swell— even I did pretty good. Boyd got a check today for $198 from a man, Mr. Crowell, who is president of the Quaker Oats Company, in Chicago, and who is going to send Boyd through school from now on. Boyd was almost crying when he told me about it; he was so happy. I think it's wonderful too. He took the el into Chicago right away to go thank Mr. Crowell. "I came here with $2.00 in my pocket and now—praise the Lord."—Boyd

WEDNESDAY, FEBRUARY 9, 1938: I am so thankful! Several were saved in the service tonight and Dr. Page preached a wonderful sermon just on taking the Lord Jesus as Savior. Boyd was with me, and going home he said, "No one ever loved me like you. No one ever did so much for me." I don't understand. I never did anything for him, and he knows I'm not in love with him.

TUESDAY, APRIL 19: Tonight Boyd is working on a talk and decorating for junior class chapel tomorrow. Then he is going to help hunt for the senior cake. I wish I could help.

WEDNESDAY, APRIL 20: Boyd spoke in chapel on the ascension, and it was wonderful. Then one of the faculty asked us if we would have our pictures taken as the typical college couple—to go on the Wheaton *Bulletin!*

MONDAY, MAY 2: A beautiful warm day, and God is good. And how I thank him for Boyd who makes me so happy. He's so kind. We walked in the woods and found a warbler and a gorgeous scarlet tanager! Sometimes I think I might be in love.

FRIDAY, MAY 13: Open lit with Boyd tonight. Last year at open lit we had our first date. Boyd sent *three dozen* roses this afternoon! There was a full moon and "Smiling Thru'" over the radio! Thank you, dear God.

SATURDAY, MAY 14: Tonight was Open House at Clark's, and Boyd was an elegant host. I'm so happy—and I really think I love Boyd. But I can't know for sure until I see Jon again.

TUESDAY, MAY 17: It's past midnight and Roomie and I are still up—she to study, and I to watch my moth come out of its cocoon. Also I'm waiting for Boyd to come by and tell me whether they've found the senior cake. It is *so* exciting! They think they know where it is!

WEDNESDAY, MAY 18: They found the cake! Boyd whistled under my window at 5:00 A.M. all dirty and happy. They'd been working all night. It was under the sidewalk by the tower, and the seniors threw water on them while they dug it up!

SUNDAY, MAY 22: The sun shone today, but it's still cold. This afternoon Boyd and I sat out on the campus, and he read out of his Greek Testament for me. I just love to have him do that.

THURSDAY, MAY 26: Being twenty isn't half as bad as I thought! The girls woke me at 12:01 A.M. and sang happy birthday! Sweet telegram from the folks. Boyd and I had a long talk about putting the Lord first in our lives.

WEDNESDAY, JUNE 8: Jinna is here—the darlin' ! She's so sweet. Mother and Grandma are coming in a few days. Roomie is packing—weep and moan—another year is almost over.

MONDAY, JUNE 13: We are now in a tourist court somewhere in Missouri. Boyd was wonderful this morning (and Grandma told him so!) and took care of everything—especially me! I bumped my head getting into the car just as we left, and he kissed it right before everyone! "God bless you, tyke," Boyd said.

By Tuesday we were home again and it almost stormed before we got there; but the Lord had kept us from harm. Dad was glad to see us and we to see him.

SATURDAY, JUNE 18: I think Jon is in town. I'm not sure because he hasn't called or anything—which is just as it should be. I'm not sorry. I do want to talk to him though.

SUNDAY, JUNE 19: I'm sure Jon didn't mean to see me, but this afternoon we were both crossing the balcony at church in the opposite directions and almost ran into each other. So we talked, and I told him that as far as I knew we were just friends and that was all. He said, "You're cute and loveable and I love you—but it fizzled." I feel awful.

MONDAY, JUNE 20: My heart ached today thinking of Jon and how he might be feeling. I pray the Lord will give him peace and joy (and me also—I need him to give them to me). Helped Dad, and read and shopped and washed dishes. Got two letters from Boyd.

At prayer meeting a deacon said, "I had the privilege of taking Jon Scott to Vernon today. I never saw a young man so completely yielded to the Lord's will." He may never know how thankful I was to hear that. I felt so much better.

TUESDAY, JULY 12: Ooooh—it's so hot—and I'm sort of tired too! I wrote Roomie and sent my preregistration fee to Wheaton. Also assigned more Little Sisters. Two letters from Boyd. He's digging post holes and driving a power buck rake (whatever that is) at the WHR ranch in Cheyenne.

SATURDAY, JULY 16: It's lightning in the north. I wrote Boyd but I didn't tell him I'm as lonely as everything and wish and wish I could just talk to him a bit. I wonder if he misses me—his letters are all jolly . . .

TUESDAY, JULY 19: Boyd called me! It was a good thing because I was dying to talk to him. Ooooh, it was wonderful! He said he missed me and loved me, and he called me the things only he calls me!

WEDNESDAY, AUGUST 31: I think I was never so glad to tear a month off the calendar as I am this one. And yet I wonder if I should be? The Lord has given me many opportunities for his service. I wish that I had used them better. I praise the Lord for this August, he has done so much for me. No matter where I am, if he wants me there, that is where I want to be.

TUESDAY, SEPTEMBER 6: I've been rushing around all day trying to pack, and it isn't done. Boyd called from Iowa to say he'd meet me in Chicago, and it was wonderful!

THURSDAY, SEPTEMBER 8: Wheaton again! A full moon! And Boyd! Dear diary, he's wonderful! He met me in Chicago and we drove to Wheaton in his folks' car. "I love you. You're beautiful." And I told him I loved him! It just sort of slipped out. But no more.

FRIDAY, SEPTEMBER 9: There's such peace in my heart—and yet —but "trust in the Lord with all thine heart and lean not on thine own understanding." Boyd asked me to marry him and I said I would—on Dow House steps, and I had on his coat because it was cool in the moonlight and the sleeves dangled down over my hands. "My Connie—mine!" He almost yelled it! And he lifted me up and swung me around and kissed me good.

SATURDAY, SEPTEMBER 10: A whole twenty-four hours of being engaged and I still want to be! We're positively keeping it a secret from everybody because, of course, we will let our parents know first. Boyd started the day for me with yellow roses and blue delphinium, and tonight we went riding for awhile in the moonlight. In between, I saw Little Sisters—met trains—got a bunch together for lunch—and played (Boyd led) for frosh songs.

We decided (or I did mostly) not to write our folks, but to tell them as soon as we saw them.

MONDAY, SEPTEMBER 12: I'm very, very tired and it's late too. My darlin' Roomie is here and I am very happy. Boyd has been swell. We went for a bit of a walk tonight. Gee! I do love him, and yes, he loves me—which takes more faith for me to say— and believe.

THURSDAY, SEPTEMBER 15: Boyd and I had dinner in Aurora. Boyd was absolutely crazy—because he is so happy, he says. So am I. He's sort of talking about a ring, and I agree. I love him— not a doubt nor fear.

No one can know how afraid I was of waking on September 10 to doubt and fear. When instead there was peace and joy, I almost could not believe it. I was to find a little more surely each day there was no rhyme nor reason to love. Love was all of grace and there was no price on its head. It was something given and not something that could be taken. The wonder of it would make a lifetime all too short.

The diary can finish the story, but it only touches on another decision we made. Boyd and I became Baptists for the second time. We joined our respective home churches when we were children. Boyd's parents were staunch Northern Baptists and loved their denomination. He told me of coming home late one evening and going into his parents' room to say good night. He did not even switch on the light, but after greeting them, he said he had been thinking about some things he would do when he became pastor of a church. For one thing, he would not require baptism for church membership.

Boyd's mother was a deaconess. In a bound, she was out of bed. She switched on the light, opened her Bible, and taught her son what the Bible said about baptism. Boyd's father added his "amen" to all she said. And Boyd decided he would do a little more thinking on the subject. Both of us had a heritage of Bible-believing, Baptist parents.

At Wheaton, Boyd, joined the Congregational "Church of Christ." It was a joy and blessing to him, but his pattern on Sundays became similar to mine.

Both of us were working in a junior church in Glen Ellyn. It was neither Baptist nor fundamentalist. It was inevitable that the pastor would ask us to come to his study after the service one morning. First, he complimented us on the good job we were doing. The children liked us and attendance was up. He did not want what he had to say to discourage us or make us feel he did not want us to stay. But some of the parents objected to their children being taught that they were unsaved. They were too young for that at the junior age. Would we please refrain from using that terminology?

I am sure we had not been presenting the gospel in the best way for the children. To tell the truth, our terminology included the word "hell." But we could say to the pastor only that unless we told the juniors a Saviour was sent into the world to save them from their sins, we had nothing to tell them at all.

As we left, I made some rather uncomplimentary remarks about the pastor's beliefs. Boyd was more charitable. "They have a right to teach what they want at their church," he said. "We are the ones who are not where we ought to be. Maybe we should go to the Baptist church at Wheaton."

We began to visit the old, red-stone church. It seemed friendlier than before. Even the music—oh well, what did that matter when things that really did matter were at stake? We found, much to our surprise, we felt at home there.

So there came a request for my church letter from First Baptist at Wheaton. Boyd and I grew to love the pastor, a graduate of Southern Baptist Seminary, and to find many friends among the citizens of Wheaton who were year-round members of the church. We were asked to help with the young people's work on Sunday evenings. We had a B.Y. group and we could teach the "good news" to them without restraint.

The spring of Boyd's senior year his major professor, Dr. Henry C. Thiessen, head of Wheaton's Bible department and a graduate of Southern Seminary, took a group of his ministerial students to Louisville. Boyd went with great eagerness. He planned to begin his seminary training the summer he graduated from Wheaton. At Louisville he inquired about opportunities to preach, and whether or not he could make his way through school and be married, too. The replies were not too enthusiastic. He had better plan to come and just take the course of study.

It happened that Dr. L. R. Scarborough, the president of Southwestern Baptist Seminary in Ft. Worth, was also visiting the Louisville campus. Boyd talked to him. Dr. Scarborough told the young man that marriage was a desirable state for a seminary student. It gave him stability and made him study harder. At Southwestern, students were encouraged to preach at every opportunity, and there were many. Boyd assured the president that he would be at Southwestern in June. Woe was him if he preached not, and he had a hankering to get married.

I had a hankering for him to get married, too. I found that by taking some extra hours and going to summer school, I could finish my college work by January, 1940. Even January, 1940, seemed a long way off in October, 1938.

TUESDAY, OCTOBER 18: Went to the concert in Chicago with Mrs. Smith. Boyd didn't go because he's saving for a ring! He has quite a bit already from his summer's work at the ranch.

SATURDAY, OCTOBER 22: Boyd and I went to Peacocks in Chicago and tried on diamond rings—I mean, I did! He says I'm getting one Christmas!

MONDAY, OCTOBER 31: What a golden October this has been! Such peace and joy the Lord has given one so unworthy as I! I didn't think I could love someone as much as I do Boyd. Today Boyd said he felt perhaps the Lord was calling him to the mission field, and I said, "I'm with you." And I am if that's where the Lord wants us.

TUESDAY, NOVEMBER 3: I've been studying French. Boyd just called and he's studying also. We talked about how we should do better for the Lord. We're so awfully happy that we almost forget everyone but ourselves. Boyd is such a rock.

THURSDAY, NOVEMBER 24: Daddy and Mother sent me the sweetest Thanksgiving telegram. After Boyd and I had dinner at the college, we spent the afternoon figuring out plans to be married and when the wedding would be. We had supper together in Dow parlor and then Boyd kissed me—not short kisses like we usually say good-night with, but real long ones.

I didn't mind. In fact, I liked it—after all we *are* engaged. But he stopped and said, "I'm not going to kiss you again like that until we are married." I was hurt, and mad too at first, but then it made me feel he was the head of the house. Which is just as it should be, so it's all right.

SUNDAY, DECEMBER 4: Boyd and I discussed the ring and we aren't sure what to do. The one we both want costs $35.00 more than Boyd has saved up, and we can't help wanting it Christmas so we can tell everyone we are engaged! Besides, it might help Daddy know we are serious.

TUESDAY, DECEMBER 6: I was too sleepy to write in this after a concert in Chicago last night, so I went to sleep and dreamed of trying and trying to earn $35.00—over and over again! I think I never wanted anything in all my life like I want that ring for Christmas.

The next day Boyd did something on impulse. He wrote his

folks and asked them to send just the $35.00 they were going to give him for the trip to Altus during Christmas. He wanted to get the ring and hitchhike to Altus! I was dazed.

FRIDAY, DECEMBER 9: Boyd came running to show me a letter from his dad saying he could have $50.00 for Christmas! But I made Boyd write and tell him he was going to hitchhike, so maybe Mr. Hunt won't. I hope not almost, because I'm scared of hitchhiking. But Boyd thinks everything is wonderful.

SUNDAY, DECEMBER 11: At noon Boyd got a special delivery letter from his folks with a *hundred* dollar check in it and two wonderful letters from them to us! They guessed everything right. Then Boyd called the man to tell him we would get the ring. We went to *The Messiah* and my heart sang with it.

But tonight when we tried to write my folks, things went wrong. Boyd wants to come home with me on the same bus or train, and I want him to, but I'm scared the folks would not like it. The Lord has done so much—maybe I should have more faith.

WEDNESDAY, DECEMBER 14: Boyd called Daddy, and he told Boyd, "Sure"—to come on with me! I can't believe it! Boyd did it because I was so worried and not eating, even though I tried to tell him I was all right. But I'm so thankful he did.

THURSDAY, DECEMBER 15: Boyd has the diamond ring! He brought it, and we skipped chapel, and I tried it on, and we looked at it and oh, it's so wonderful, but not nearly as wonderful as our love! We call the ring our rainbow—a promise from the Lord that he will always do exceeding abundantly above all we can ask or think!

FRIDAY, DECEMBER 16: I'm packing, and tomorrow Boyd and I will leave for Altus—Boyd and I! It seems like a dream.

SATURDAY, DECEMBER 17: On the bus—riding, going home for Christmas, and Boyd by my side. What will the folks do? And say? Surely the Lord is with us. I'm wearing the ring now, and it sparkles in the lights of the bus—but I'll take it off until we talk to the folks.

SUNDAY, DECEMBER 18: The ring is on my finger—with the

folks' permission! Mom is wonderful—Daddy is not so happy. After they said it was all right, Boyd said (in front of them), "Will you marry me?" and I said, "Yes, I will," and he put it on my finger.

Later, Daddy asked me how Boyd could get me a ring like this one. I told him Boyd got it with money he saved up from working on the ranch, except $35.00 which Boyd's dad sent him. And that seemed to impress Daddy more than all Boyd saved up! He said, "What parents won't do for their children!"

WEDNESDAY, DECEMBER 21: Boyd and I went to prayer meeting and everyone was swell. I showed them my ring, and they liked it. They liked Boyd, too, and they were surprised. I saw some of the men looking at Boyd, and then they came up and told Daddy he was a fine young man. Daddy just shook his head and said, "Oh Lordy!"

SATURDAY, DECEMBER 31: How shocked I am to find that another year has passed! Of course, it's the very best I have ever had—or it seems to me—'though I'm sure the Lord made the others like they were so this one would be like it has been. How thankful I am.

TUESDAY, APRIL 11, 1939: Dear ole diary: Boyd loves me and wants to be my husband. I love him and want to be his wife. But we can't be that now. So I cried when I got an O.U. bulletin and thought about being away from him all summer and fall.

FRIDAY, JUNE 2: Boyd is graduating in *absentia* (And is that ever hard per to get!) and will leave tomorrow to enrol in Southwestern Seminary for the summer session. I was elected president of Ladies tonight— mainly due to Roomie. They were swell. Roomie is happy and so dear. She calls Boyd her "Roomie-in-law!"

MONDAY, JUNE 12: In Norman at O.U., and one day of school is over. It won't be too hard, I think. Mom got me two new dresses and they're so nice. Got a letter from Boyd and he really likes the seminary. If Southwestern were a girl instead of a school, I'd be jealous!

SUNDAY, SEPTEMBER 10: Boyd was ordained at his church in Oklahoma today. He was so sincere, and I was proud of him. His folks surprised him and came from Iowa to see it. They are here at our house now, and Daddy and Mother make me so happy by playing the perfect hosts.

FRIDAY, SEPTEMBER 15: Wheaton! I'm all unpacked and at my own dear desk. But, oh, how strange not to have Boyd waiting at Union Station! I miss him. But it's great to be here except for that.

SATURDAY, SEPTEMBER 23: Little Sister tea this afternoon, and I smiled and shook hands for hours in the reception line. Ladosian rendevouz this evening, and it was such fun around the fire. I long, long, long for Boyd.

MONDAY, OCTOBER 16: Boyd phoned tonight, and another half-time church, at Charlie, Texas, called him as their pastor. And he wants to set the wedding date in February!! Oh, I'm so thankful the Lord has given him the church. It makes me all humble inside. It's still an awful little to get married on, but I'd love to— I want to!

THURSDAY, OCTOBER 26: Tonight we gave Clara, who has just become engaged, a shower; and just when we got her good and wet they began to put *me* in!!! And I'd already been in once!

SATURDAY, NOVEMBER 4: This day has been filled with cleaning and writing letters. Mostly because I got one from Mom saying Dad was the same as he was Christmas about not wanting to plan the wedding. I've written him.

TUESDAY, NOVEMBER 7: I got three letters from Boyd, but I so long to be with him. I wish almost I didn't miss him so. He's so busy I reckon he doesn't miss me too much. Besides, I'm almost scared (though I shouldn't be because the Lord knows) of what's happening at home when Dad gets my letter.

TUESDAY, NOVEMBER 14: I got a letter from Dad. He said he would cooperate with my marriage plans in spite of his personal feelings. Those last words made me cry all alone in my practice room. He just does not want me to get married yet. What shall I do now? I do not know but the Lord does.

THURSDAY, NOVEMBER 16: Today I got a letter from Jon saying he was engaged to be married and was very happy and very much in love. I'm so thankful. It was a dear letter, and I pray he may have every blessing. Boyd's letter was so full of strength, and I needed it so because I haven't heard from Mom since Daddy's letter.

FRIDAY, NOVEMBER 17: I got a swell and dear letter from Mom and have sent her a special. Boyd's was swell as usual. I have a headache because I didn't have time to eat dinner.

TUESDAY, NOVEMBER 21: My heart is full of joy. Dad sent me a letter which sounds like I am going to have a wedding and that he wants it so. The Lord seems to be bearing me up on eagle's wings.

SATURDAY, DECEMBER 9: Got a wonderful letter from Mom O.K.'ing the list of the wedding party. Then this afternoon, I went to a tea Ellen was giving and it turned out to be a shower for me! Not the wet kind—the gift kind! It was so exciting! I'd love to call Boyd.

TUESDAY, DECEMBER 19: I'm packing again—the fourth year that I've packed to go home for Christmas. Next year, Lord willing, I'll be with Boyd in our own home.

Our wedding date, February 23, was announced at a family dinner, and then Mother and Daddy gave a reception. Loads of dear people came! But dearest of all was Boyd who stood by my side and looked as if he was proud to be there. I was so proud of him!

Daddy had a talk with him about considering going into diplomatic service, and said he had some connections with Cordell Hull. Surely Daddy knows that nothing could keep Boyd from being a preacher!

MONDAY, JANUARY 1, 1940: I'm back in Wheaton and very sleepy. Boyd called and said Allan is coming from Boston to be best man! I'm so glad. Mom wrote that they'd ordered 250 invitations. Mable sent taffeta and tulle. Roomie said she'd come for sure.

THURSDAY, JANUARY 11: I played in the conservatory recital

tonight. People said nice things. Mr. Van Dusen stayed on the campus for the recital because it was my last time. He said I played the Chopin Nocturne as well as anything he had heard done by a Wheaton student! From him that is solid rubies, and I'm going to put it away in my mind somewhere so I can remember it when I'm old. Mr. Stam liked the Chopin scherzo, and I really appreciated that. He also said I was recommended for honors!

FRIDAY, JANUARY 19: This morning in political science class Dr. Edman asked Clarence to get a book, and he came back with a big package. It was a rolling pin for me! It was fun, and we had cocoa and doughnuts afterwards.

SUNDAY, JANUARY 21: People were wonderful to me at the Baptist church today. At B.Y. Francis gave me a little gold necklace and said, "If it hadn't been for you I wouldn't have loved the Lord Jesus." That makes me want to cry. Boyd wrote the dearest letter.

TUESDAY, JANUARY 30: Mom and I went to Ft. Worth today, and Boyd and I picked out the apartment. It's swell. It needs curtains, and they will be fun to fix. Also Boyd had the wedding ring!

SUNDAY, FEBRUARY 11: Boyd came yesterday, and we've had a wonderful time. I shall never forget how lovely the stars were last night, and how I felt just being with him. Next time he comes, he'll stay till I'm his wife forever and ever.

Deep down in my heart I hoped the Lord would delay his second coming until after February 23. Wedding presents were pouring in, and I think most of them meant even more to Mother and Daddy (and to Mr. and Mrs. Hunt) than to Boyd and me. "This came from the Stephensons in Dallas," Mother told Daddy as she showed him one gift.

"Well, who'd have thought they'd do that?" Daddy said wonderingly.

The Tennessee Moores sent an antique chair, and Boyd's cousin Lucile, in Detroit, sent a Wedgewood bowl which we thought so beautiful we began getting china to match it. I wrote thank-you notes right to February 22, and then gave up until after the wedding.

Friday, the twenty-third, was one of those warm days that come once every February in Oklahoma. Mother had the windows pushed up and did not try to keep the doors closed, which was a good thing. There was hardly a minute someone was not going in or out. The sky was blue, and there were some little, fleecy, white clouds like the lambs you see on calendars.

Alberta and Marguerite and Roomie and Clarence helped decorate a trellis, which was to go in front of the baptistry, with gallons of ivy. Some fellows came up from Seminary Hill resolved to kidnap Boyd for a few hours, but they never did find him. Boyd was with me while I went to every store in town looking for white-satin slippers. At the last minute we discovered that the pair I was supposed to have had not arrived. It took all afternoon, and we reveled in the time together. There was so much going on at home and at the church, we hardly saw each other anyhow.

We got home just as Mother was about to serve buffet supper to everyone. Boyd and I were not hungry. Our mothers fixed Baptist eggnogs and brought the glasses upstairs to our rooms. Boyd said he drank his; I took two good sips of mine.

Since Boyd and the ushers were wearing tuxes, we rented one for Daddy. David and Fred said they were going to charge twenty-five cents admission at the church door from people who would get to see Daddy coming down the aisle in a tux. But Daddy was acting up again about my getting married. He said he would pay the bills for the wedding, but even if we got a thousand tuxes, he was not going to walk down that aisle and give his daughter away. Somebody could take her, but he was not giving.

We took that part out of the ceremony, and told him he could just take me down the aisle and there would be no mention of "who gives this woman?" He said he still would not touch that tux and was not going down the aisle.

Late in the afternoon, Mr. Hunt went to Daddy's office and they talked. No one knows to this day what they said to each other, but Daddy came home and put on the tuxedo without a word. Mother, her eyes snapping, said she *imagined* Mr. Hunt told him it was not so easy to give up a *son* either.

Daddy took me down the church aisle. Boyd was waiting at the front. I had dreamed of his watching me come down the aisle as he would a delicate Dresden doll, his expression one of adoring concern. Instead, he looked at me with somewhat the same expression he gets on his face when he sees a banana-cream pie baked just for him. When people speak of being at our wedding, they still say what they remember best is that smile on Boyd's face. It was more of a grin.

Boyd came to the beginning of the aisle to meet me, which was a good thing, because Daddy got only as far as the second pew from the front where Mother was sitting. He stopped there, took my arm from his, and in an awkward, loving motion placed it in the one Boyd offered. Then he sat down by Mother and rubbed his hand over his head.

Boyd and I memorized our vows so we could turn and say them to each other.

"I, Boyd, take thee, Connie . . ."

"I, Connie, take thee, Boyd . . ."

We did not miss a single word except Boyd said "to have and to hold" twice.

While we stood there together in the candlelight, Roberta sang "Because." When she got to "because God made thee mine, I'll cherish thee," Boyd looked down at me as if I were something far better than a Dresden doll.

My path had joined another which for most of my life I had not even known was there, and now they led as one path through valleys and over hills, as far ahead as we could see.

At the wedding reception, the gayest one was Daddy. Mother said she would never forgive him for causing her so much worry about the wedding and then enjoying it so much, but, of course, she did. The house was filled with friends of many years, and

Daddy jovially accepted their teasing about losing a daughter—and to a Yankee and a preacher at that!

"That's what you get for sending her so far away to school," Dr. Abernathy said.

"Boyd's the one I feel sorry for," said Daddy. "It's too late for him to back out now. I did everything I could to help him get away, but he's a goner." Mr. Hunt clapped him on the back and laughed with the rest.

After the wild ride to get away, we called our parents to thank them and assure them we had arrived safely at our destination. I talked to Daddy and he said, "Oh, I wasn't a bit worried. I knew Boyd would take care of you."

There came a time when Mother told me that, years before, he said to her, "When Connie really makes up her mind, nobody —not us or anyone else—will be able to keep her from getting married and leaving home."

Mother understood. "But our children are still our children, no matter where they are," she said.

"And our home is always their home," said Daddy.

Postlude

On Saturday night we finally persuaded Mother to go home for a little rest. Early Sunday morning David, Larry, Virginia, Boyd, and I were in the room beside Daddy. He had been unconscious for several days. Boyd and David were having a scientific-theological discussion about when birth and death actually occur.

They were getting very technical when Larry spoke. "I don't care what you say. A person isn't dead until he's drawn the last breath in his body."

We looked at Daddy and felt our emotions slipping out of control. To cover up, David told a joke. We kept the jokes going for awhile.

Suddenly, David heard what he was really listening for. Daddy made a slight sound, something like a sigh. David sprang to his side. "This is it," he said.

We fell silent while David used his stethoscope, and lifted Daddy's eyelid. He pulled the needles of the intravenous feedings from Daddy's arms. "I'm glad he doesn't have to have those anymore," he choked.

Daddy had hated them. He submitted to them only when David told him it must be. He had hated the hospital bed too. He had tried to leave it to go walking outside awhile. I wished he could have left it and walked outside—yes, even if he walked on until he fell to die under the stars or the wind or the sun. That would have suited Daddy far better than "civilized" dying.

Moses got to die right. He climbed a mountain and no one found him but God.

Someone went to get Mother, and someone else called an ambulance. Mother was the steady one, the rock. "I knew he wanted me to go home last night," she said. "When we were at the office he always said, 'Now, Mother, you go on home so I can lock up,' and I guess that's the way he wanted it this time."

We wept. At home, I heard David's racking sobs coming from his bedroom.

When I first saw Daddy lying in his casket, he looked so good —so much more like himself than he had on his deathbed. My heart sang out, "Hi, Daddy!" But there was no answer. Death is hard.

At the funeral, the pastor told us things about Daddy that we had never known. Daddy probably would have pretended to wonder who was being talked about. We marveled at the comfort our friends gave us. Boyd's and my hearts bounded when we saw the Summers and President and Mrs. Head from the seminary attending the funeral. We were overwhelmed at the flowers and phone calls and telegrams from Houston. Altus seemed filled with compassionate friends. Anita, David's wife, insisted on coming, even though she was expecting their third child. Daddy's brothers flew in from Tennessee—Uncle Doc, Uncle Henry, Uncle Holt, Uncle Fred. Daddy's Tennesseans were there.

And Daddy, who had not thought he would live to see his children grown, would have enjoyed his grandchildren at the funeral. The oldest one wiped tears away and the youngest fell asleep.

Daddy was buried beside his infant, first-born son, under the tall cedar tree he had planted there for shade. The pastor read the twenty-third Psalm, and we all went home.

It was almost twilight when Boyd and I and the children drove across the Red River bridge that took us from Oklahoma into Texas. I looked back at the soft-blue sky reaching down to earth and thought, "How rich you are tonight, Oklahoma soil! There is some of Tennessee in you, some of Galveston's wind and sea, untold yearning for what Dallas meant, and years and years of Oklahoma toil."

I did not say that Daddy was there. Daddy was a deacon, a man who worked six days of the week and sang on Sunday. I figured he was working now, and singing too—on tune:

> Amazing grace! how sweet the sound,
> That saved a wretch like me!
> I once was lost, but now am found,
> Was blind, but now I see.